Edexcel GCSE
Religious Studies

Unit 9
Christianity

Jane Kelly

A PEARSON COMPANY

Published by Pearson Education Limited, a company incorporated in England and Wales, having its registered office at Edinburgh Gate, Harlow, Essex, CM20 2JE. Registered company number: 872828

www.heinemann.co.uk

Edexcel is a registered trade mark of Edexcel Limited

Text © Pearson Ltd 2009
First published 2009

13 12 11 10 09
10 9 8 7 6 5 4 3 2 1

British Library Cataloguing in Publication Data
A catalogue record for this book is available from the British Library.

ISBN 978 1 846904 24 0

Edited by Florence Production Ltd, Stoodleigh, Devon
Designed by HL Studios, Long Hanborough, Oxford
Typeset by HL Studios, Long Hanborough, Oxford
Produced by Florence Production Ltd, Stoodleigh, Devon
Original illustrations © Pearson Education Ltd 2009
Illustrated by HL Studios
Cover design by Pearson Education Ltd
Picture research by Zooid Pictures
Cover photo/illustration © Mike Binner /Alamy
Printed in Spain by Graficas

Acknowledgements
The authors and publisher would like to thank the following individuals and organisations for permission to reproduce photographs:

Adel Nassief, p. 12; Alamy pp. 33, 65; Andrew F. Kazmierski/Shutterstock p. 73; Antonia Rolls pp. 2–3; ArkReligion.com/Alamy pp. 54, 67; Ateliers et Presses de Taizé, 71250 Taizé, France pp. 22–23; BBC Photograph Library/Tiger Aspect Productions, p. 50; Bill Asprey/Tribune Media Services p. 16; Bob Edme/Associated Press/Press Association Images, p. 47; Brendan Powell Smith/www.thebricktestament.com, pp. 70, 102; British Library/akg-images, p. 34; c.Universal/Everett/Rex Features, p. 94; Children's Society, p. 114; Claudio Peri/Epa/Corbis UK Ltd., p. 49; Corbis UK Ltd., pp. 110–111; CountrySideCollection/Homer Sykes/Alamy, p. 17; Courtesy of Diocese of Saint Augustine Office of Vocations, p. 96; dbimages/Alamy, p. 18; Deshakalyan Chowdhury/AFP/Getty Images, p. 25; Electa/akg-images, p. 36; Enric Marti/Associated Press/Press Association Images, p. 41; Eric Thomas/dkimages.com, p. 37; Erich Lessing/akg-images, p. 63; Erich Lessing/Musée du Louvre/akg-images, p. 83; eye ubiquitous/Robert Harding Picture Library, p. 62; Francisco Amaral Leitão/Shutterstock, p. 85; Howard Davies/Corbis UK Ltd., p. 92; Image Source Ltd, p. 23; imagebroker/Alamy, p. 5; INTERFOTO/Alamy, p. 10; iStockphoto, pp. 82, 95; ITV/Rex Features, p. 69; Jeremy Hoare/Life File/Photolibrary Group, p. 55; jon le-bon/Shutterstock, p. 21; Jules Selmes/Pearson Education, p. 23; Justin Williams/Rex Features, p. 39; Karim Jaafar/AFP/Getty Images, p. 99; Kevin Peterson/© Photodisc. 1998, p. 23; Kevin Peterson/© Photodisc. 1999, p. 23; © Kim Karpeles/Alamy, p. 72; M. Freeman/Photodisc, p. 9; Marco Di Lauro/Getty Images, p. 97; Maria Bobrova/Shutterstock, p. 6; Mary Evans Picture Library/Alamy, p. 77; MASSIMO MERLINI/Shutterstock, p. 43; mehmet alci/Shutterstock, p. 105; Nicolas McComber/iStockphoto, p. 46; Photo Scala, Florence, p. 100; Photo12.com, pp. 90–91; Photographers Direct/Jim and Mary Whitmer, p. 71; Photolink/© Photodisc. 1999, p. 72; Photolink/Photodisc, p. 68; Pontino/Alamy, p. 51; Press Association Images, pp. 35, 45, 76, 81, 95, 106; Quentin Bargate/Alamy, p. 26; ReligiousStock/Alamy, p. 42; Reuters/Corbis UK Ltd., p. 20; Revd Henriette and Toby Howarth/The Church of England, p. 52; Robert Glusic Photography/Photodisc, p. 8; Robert Harding Picture Library Ltd/Alamy, p. 80; Robin Bryant/The Salvation Army, p. 115; RubberBall/Alamy, p. 38; The Salvation Army, pp. 71, 112; Samaritans, p. 19; Sergey I/Shutterstock, pp. 60–61; shutterstock, p. 72; Sipa Press/Rex Features, pp. 48, 108; Steve Allen Travel Photography/Alamy, p. 72; Ted Soqui/Corbis, p. 74; Time Life Pictures/Mansell/Getty Images, p. 40; TNT Magazine/Alamy, p. 70; Tom Carter/Photolibrary Group, p. 64; TravelStockCollection/Homer Sykes/Alamy, p. 75; Tudor Photography/© Pearson Education Ltd. 2005, p. 72; Universal Pictures/Album/akg-images, p. 4; Valerie Gill/The Fairtrade Foundation, p. 27; Warner Bros. Pictures/Album/akg-images, p. 14; www.jonathanfalk.com/Jonathan Falk, p. 109.

Every effort has been made to contact copyright holders of material reproduced in this book. Any omissions will be rectified in subsequent printings if notice is given to the publishers.

The author would also like to thank Richard and her parents for all their support and encouragement over the years

Websites
There are links to relevant websites in this book. In order to ensure that the links are up to date, that the links work, and that the sites are not inadvertently linked to sites that could be considered offensive, we have made the links available on the Heinemann website at www.heinemann.co.uk/hotlinks. When you access the site, the express code is 4240P.

Disclaimer
This material has been published on behalf of Edexcel and offers high-quality support for the delivery of Edexcel qualifications.
This does not mean that the material is essential to achieve any Edexcel qualification, nor does it mean it is the only suitable material available to support any Edexcel qualification. Edexcel material will not be used verbatim in setting any Edexcel examination or assessment. Any resource lists produced by Edexcel shall include this and other appropriate texts.

Copies of official specifications for all Edexcel qualifications may be found on the Edexcel website – www.edexcel.com

Contents

Welcome to this Edexcel GCSE in Religious Studies Resource

These resources have been written to support fully Edexcel's new specification for GCSE Religious Studies. Each Student Book covers one unit of the specification which makes up a Short Course qualification. Any two units from separate modules of the specification make up a Full Course qualification. Written by experienced examiners, and packed with exam tips and activities, these books include lots of engaging features to enthuse students and provide the range of support needed to make teaching and learning a success for all ability levels.

Features in this book

In each section you will find the following features:

- **an introductory spread** which introduces the topics and gives the Edexcel key terms and learning outcomes for the whole section

- **topic spreads** containing the following features:

  - **Learning outcomes** for the topic

    edexcel ::: key terms

    Specification key terms – are emboldened and defined for easy reference

  - **Activities** and **For discussion** panels provide stimulating tasks for the classroom and homework

  - a topic **Summary** captures the main learning points.

How to use this book

Throughout the series the New International Bible has been used.

This book has been written to support Edexcel Religious Studies GCSE Module C Unit 9 Christianity. However, please note that religions other than Christianity can be studied for this exam.

This book is split into the four sections of the specification.

A dedicated suite of revision resources for complete exam success. We've broken down the six stages of revision to ensure that you are prepared every step of the way.

How to get into the perfect 'zone' for your revision.

Tips and advice on how to plan your revision effectively.

Revision activities and exam-style practice at the end of every section plus additional exam practice at the end of the book.

Last-minute advice for just before the exam.

An overview of what you will have to do in the exam, plus a chance to see what a real exam paper will look like.

What do you do after your exam? This section contains information on how to get your results and answers to frequently asked questions on what to do next.

ResultsPlus

These features are based on how students have performed in past exams. They are combined with expert advice and guidance from examiners to show you how to achieve better results.

There are four different types of ResultsPlus features throughout this book:

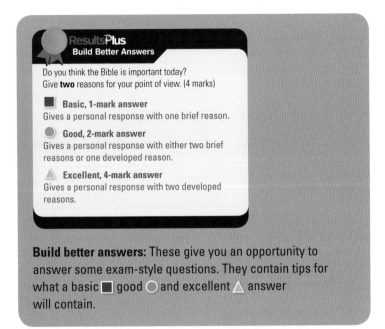

Build better answers: These give you an opportunity to answer some exam-style questions. They contain tips for what a basic ■ good ○ and excellent △ answer will contain.

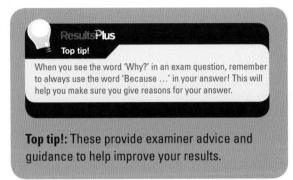

Top tip!: These provide examiner advice and guidance to help improve your results.

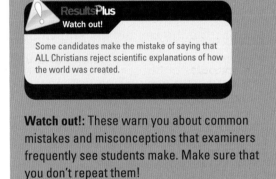

Watch out!: These warn you about common mistakes and misconceptions that examiners frequently see students make. Make sure that you don't repeat them!

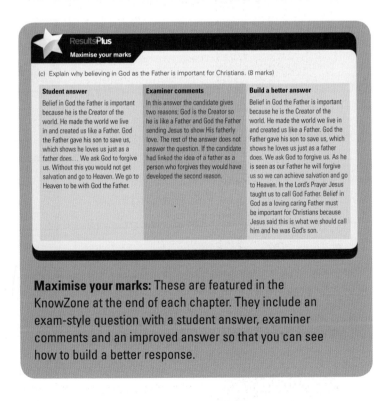

Maximise your marks: These are featured in the KnowZone at the end of each chapter. They include an exam-style question with a student answer, examiner comments and an improved answer so that you can see how to build a better response.

Beliefs and values

Introduction

In this section you will explore, think and learn about the beliefs and values that are important to Christians.

Learning outcomes for this section

By the end of this section, you should be able to:

- give definitions of the key terms and use them in answer to GCSE questions
- describe the key beliefs and values of Christianity
- explain why the key beliefs and values are important for Christians
- express your own point of view about the key beliefs and values of the Christian faith, giving your reasons
- evaluate points of view about the key beliefs and values of the Christian faith, showing that you have thought about different views from your own, giving reasons and evidence
- describe the meaning and importance for Christians of believing in God as Unity, Trinity, Father and Creator
- describe the meaning and importance for Christians of believing Jesus is the Son of God
- describe the meaning and importance for Christians of believing in the Holy Spirit
- describe the meaning and importance of Christian beliefs about salvation from sin
- describe the meaning and importance of loving God and how it affects a Christian's life
- describe the meaning and importance of Christian teachings on the love of others
- explain how love for God and others is expressed in the life of a religious community
- explain how a Christian church shows love for God and others in the local area.

edexcel ▦ key terms

atonement	creeds	monotheism	Trinity
catechism	faith	repentance	Unity
compassion	incarnation	salvation	Virgin Birth

Fascinating fact

Of the world's population, 33 per cent is Christian. It is the largest world religion. In the 2001 UK census 37.3 million people in England and Wales said they were Christians.

1 Describe what you see in this picture.

2 What message do you think the artist is trying to get across?

3 Read Matthew 28:18–20. How do you think this passage relates to the picture?

4 What do you think are the key Christian beliefs?

5 What does it mean to have a faith today?

1.1 God as Unity and Trinity

Learning outcomes

By the end of this lesson you should be able to:

- describe the meaning of Unity, Trinity and monotheism
- give your own opinion, with a reason, about God as Unity and Trinity
- explain why the belief in God as Unity and Trinity is important to Christians
- evaluate the importance of the belief in God as Unity and Trinity for Christians.

edexcel ⠿ key terms

Creeds – Statements of Christian belief.

Monotheism – Belief in one God.

Trinity – The belief that God is three in one.

Unity – God's way of being one.

Unity and Trinity – three in one

Unity means being one. For Christians, God is Unity because there is only one God and everything in the universe comes from him.

Even though Christians believe in the Unity of God, they believe God makes himself known to the world as a **Trinity**: the Father, the Son and the Holy Spirit.

The Holy Spirit who inspires, gives strength and brings God into people's lives

The Father who created the universe

The Son who was God on Earth and who saves people from sin

St Patrick (the patron saint of Ireland) used the image of the shamrock to explain the Trinity. He said it was a plant with one stem, but it has three leaves; just as God is three in one.

Morgan Freeman played God in the film Bruce Almighty.

For discussion

Think of five words that might be used to describe God.

Activities

1 Imagine you have been asked to explain a difficult idea like electricity to a younger person. In pairs, work out how you would explain it. You can use words, pictures and/or drama.

2 Think of three ways you might explain the idea of the Unity of God. Explain why you have chosen them.

The nature of God

When people talk about the nature of God, they are describing what God is like. It is very hard to describe God – it is difficult to describe what you cannot see. So Christians use a variety of words and ideas to explain what they believe about God. All Christians believe in one God; this is called **monotheism**.

For discussion

Do you think God should be described as Unity?

Why Christians believe God is One

The universe itself shows oneness. Christians believe that everything in it has a unique pattern, showing that it must have been created by only one person – God.

The Bible teaches that there is only one God. The first of the Ten Commandments says there is only one God. When Jesus was asked which was the Greatest Commandment, he said 'the Lord our God, the Lord is One'.

The **creeds** teach that there is only one God. The Nicene Creed starts with the words 'We believe in one God.'

For discussion

How does the column below show the idea of the Trinity? Do you think the Trinity can be truly represented as a picture, statue or image?

'Three cannot be One.' Do you agree?

The Holy Trinity Column in the Czech Republic.

Why Christians believe in the Trinity

In Genesis, the first book of the Old Testament, it says 'And God said, let us make man in our own likeness…'. Who is 'us'? Christians believe it is a reference to the Trinity; three persons in one.

When Jesus was baptised, the three aspects of the Trinity were present – the Father, the Son and Holy Spirit (look at the topic on infant baptism, on pages 62–63, for more about this).

When Jesus commissioned the disciples he referred to the Trinity and told them to go and baptise in the name of the Father, Son and Holy Spirit.

The Trinity is a key teaching of the Christian Church. All the creeds speak of one God seen in three aspects: the Father, the Son and Holy Spirit.

Activities

3   Ice, water and steam have been used to help people understand what the Trinity is. Explain how this would help people to understand.

4   Why is the Trinity so important to Christians today?

ResultsPlus
Build better answers

What is monotheism? (2 marks)

■   **Poor, 0-mark answers**
Gives a definition of another key term.

●   **Basic, 1-mark answers**
Gives a partially correct answer – for example, 'Belief in God'.

▲   **Good, 2-mark answers**
Gives the glossary definition or uses alternative wording – for example, 'Belief in one God'.

Summary

• Christians believe there is only one God.
• Unity is God's way of being one.
• Christians believe that God can be known in three ways: the Father, the Son, the Holy Spirit. This is known as the Trinity.

1.2 God as the Father

Learning outcomes

By the end of this lesson you should be able to:

- describe the meaning of the term 'catechism'
- give your own opinion, with a reason, about God as Father
- explain why the belief in God as Father is important to Christians
- evaluate the importance of the belief in God as Father for Christians.

For discussion

Look at the photograph. What makes someone a father? What should a father provide and what are his responsibilities to the child?

edexcel ▦ key terms

Catechism – Official teaching of the Roman Catholic Church.

God as Father

The term 'Father' is used to describe God. Just as a father on Earth provides for his child's needs, God provides for his children's needs too. An Earthly father loves and wants to protect his child from danger, just like God. An Earthly father can let his children down, but God does not.

A personal God

Jesus taught his disciples to call God 'Abba', the word for father in Jesus's time. A father is the person who both creates and sustains life. Because of this there is a unique loving bond between the father and the child. Christians see God as someone they can relate to and someone who cares for them no matter what they do, just like the best parents do for their child.

Activities

1   Imagine you have just become a father for the first time. Write a letter to your newborn son or daughter telling them what you hope to do for them.

For discussion

What makes someone a good parent?

The Lord's Prayer

Jesus taught his followers to refer to God as Father, in the Lord's Prayer. Christians all over the world recite it and it is the prayer that is most often used in public and private worship. The opening words of the prayer are 'Our Father'. This emphasises that God is Father to all humans and that he created and is father to the whole world. Jesus called God 'father' and encouraged his followers to do the same. This shows that God can be approached in the same way that a child would approach a loving parent.

God as the Father almighty

The Apostles' Creed starts with the words 'I believe in God, the Father almighty…' The idea of the Father being almighty is important. The idea of 'father' tells us of the personal relationship humans can have with God, while 'almighty' draws attention to the fact that God is the all-powerful Father and nothing is beyond his authority.

For Roman Catholics (see page 6), the **Catechism** teaches that, by calling God 'Father,' Christians are acknowledging that God is the origin of everything and has the greatest authority. Yet at the same time it is a way of remembering that God has loving care for all his children.

Sacred texts

'The Lord's Prayer' (Luke 11:1–4)

'God as Father' (2 Corinthians 6:18)

Activities

2 Read 'A Father's love letter'. What qualities of fatherhood does it show? Make a list.
3 Explain why Christians call God 'Father'.
4 Find out what the Apostles's Creed teaches Christians.
5 What is the Catechism? Why is it important for Catholics?

A Father's love letter

My Child,

You may not know me, but I know everything about you. I created you and in my image. I am not a stranger to you, I love you because you are my child and I am your Father. I am always thinking of you and encouraging you to do good. I will be your teacher and guide through life. When you are in need I will be there to comfort you. I love you even as I love my son, Jesus.

I will always be your Father.

Activities

Challenge

6 What idea of God does the following quotation give?

'Can a mother forget the baby at her breast
And have no compassion on the child she has borne?
Though she may forget,
I will not forget,
See I have engraved you on my hand…'
(Isaiah 49:15–16)

For discussion

'Calling God "Father" is outdated in today's world.' Do you agree?

Summary

- Christians call God 'Father' as they believe he created them, cares for them and guides them.
- Jesus referred to God as his father and taught his followers to pray using the prayer 'Our Father'.
- The Creeds and catechism refer to God as Father.

1.3 God as the Creator

Learning outcomes

By the end of this lesson you should be able to:

- describe the meaning of the term 'Creator'
- give your own opinion, with a reason, about God as Creator
- explain why the belief in God as Creator is important to Christians
- evaluate the importance of the belief in God as Creator for Christians.

The Creation story in Genesis

In God's own image

God created human beings last and in God's own image. This makes human beings special; as they are capable of having a spiritual relationship with God. With this special relationship comes the responsibility of looking after all of God's creation.

God as Creator

Christians look at the world around them and see both the beauty and complexity of nature. Christians believe that the creation of the world was not an accident; but that there is a Creator who created the universe. The Creator is God. God is the Creator of all things. As God is good, so is the world he created.

Sacred texts

'The story of Creation' (Genesis Chapter 1)

'God's glory is revealed in the universe' (Psalms 19:1)

Activities

1   Find three pictures from nature and explain how Christians could use them to show how God must be the Creator of the universe.

2   Design a poster or PowerPoint® presentation illustrating the Creation story in Genesis.

For discussion

How would you describe this scene above to a friend who hasn't seen it? Choose five words that you think best summarise the picture.

Do you think God should be described as the Creator?

Different Christian views on the story of Creation

Some Christians believe the story of Creation, as told in Genesis, to be literally true, since the Bible is the word of God. Therefore, they do not accept the scientific view. These Christians are often called 'Creationists'. Other Christians believe that the story is not a factually accurate account, but is symbolic, and just gives an overview of Creation. They believe the Bible was inspired by God, but the writers used their own words.

Many Christians agree with the 'big bang' theory as the explanation of how God created the world. They believe science answers the question of *how* the world started, but the Creation story tells us *why* it was created.

Activities

Challenge

3   The human genome is one of the most important scientific discoveries in recent years. Try to find out more about this. Do you think this supports or rejects the idea of God as Creator?

Why God as Creator is important for Christians

- The Creation story shows that God is all powerful, omnipotent, as he created everything.
- As God created the world it shows that it is important to him, and there is a purpose behind it and to our existence.
- As God is the Creator of life it is sacred and should be respected, since God created humans in his own image.
- The Apostles' Creed states that God is the the Creator of Heaven and Earth. This is a key Christian teaching.

ResultsPlus
Watch out!

Some candidates make the mistake of saying that ALL Christians reject scientific explanations of how the world was created.

The scientific view

The 'big bang' theory

This says that the universe started with a massive explosion of matter, creating the solar system, including the Earth.

Evolution

This is the process by which life started and continues to develop on Earth. Through the process of evolution it is those that are best equipped for their environment that survive to pass on their genes to the next generations – the survival of the fittest.

Activities

4   Write or record a conversation between two Christians who hold different views about the Creation.

5   Explain why it is important for Christians to believe in a God who is the Creator of the world.

6   Find out about a scientist who is a Christian and their view on Creation.

For discussion

'Christians should believe God created the world in six days.' Do you agree?

Summary

- Christians believe that God is the Creator of the universe.
- The story in the first chapter of Genesis tells how God created the universe in six days.
- Christians have different beliefs about the Creation story. Some believe it is literally true. Others accept the scientific view – they believe that God was responsible for the Creation of the world, but that it did not happen in six days.
- Christians believe that humans were created in the image of God, and therefore that human life is sacred.

1.4 Jesus as the Son of God

Learning outcomes

By the end of this lesson you should be able to:

- describe the meaning of the Virgin Birth and the incarnation
- give your own opinion, with reasons, about the idea of Jesus as the Son of God
- explain why the belief in Jesus as the Son of God is important to Christians
- evaluate the importance of the belief in Jesus as the Son of God for Christians.

edexcel ⠿ key terms

Incarnation – The belief that God took human form in Jesus.

Virgin Birth – The belief that Jesus was not conceived through sex.

Sacred texts

'The birth of Jesus' (Luke 2:1–15 and Matthew 1:18–2:18)

'Jesus's ascension into Heaven' (Acts 1:11)

Jesus was born as God's Son

Christians believe that Jesus is the Son of God the Father. Mary gave birth to him in the normal way. Mary became pregnant through the power of the Holy Spirit. Jesus is the Son of God as he is both divine (of God) and human, because he was born to Mary, a human. This event is known as the **Virgin Birth**.

Jesus suffered as God's Son

Jesus was a real person who really did suffer and die; he was crucified. Jesus lived at a time when the Romans were ruling over Israel. Crucifixion was a Roman death penalty. As Jesus lived as a human, he felt the pain and suffering as humans do.

Jesus was resurrected as God's Son

On the third day after his death Jesus rose from the dead. As only God has the power to rise from the dead, this showed that Jesus was divine – that he was God's Son. Then he ascended to Heaven to be with his father and sit in a position of honour at his right-hand side.

For discussion

Look at the picture. Can you identify the different people in this picture of the Nativity? What message do you think it conveys about Jesus?

For discussion

'The Virgin Birth is just a story.' Do you agree?

Activities

1   Read the Apostles's Creed and pick out any statements about Jesus. Summarise each of them and draw a symbol or image beside each statement to help you remember what they are.

2   Explain how Jesus's birth, death and resurrection show Christians both his human and god-like nature.

Why the incarnation is important to Christians

Christians believe that God became a human as Jesus. This is called the **incarnation**.

The incarnation is important because:

- It means that God was Jesus's father and shows his divine nature.
- It shows that Jesus is human, as he was born in the normal way to Mary.
- It is part of the teachings of the Church. In the Apostles's Creed it states that the Virgin Mary became pregnant through the power of the Holy Spirit and gave birth to Jesus.

Activities

Challenge

3   Read John 1:1–14. There are a lot of ideas about the incarnation in this passage. Make a list of them. What does this passage tell us about why Jesus was born?

Write your own summary of what you think the term 'incarnation' means in the form of a text message.

Why the death and suffering of Jesus are important

- Jesus's death showed that God loved the world so much he was willing to give up his only son.
- As Jesus was human he felt pain and suffering just as other people do. This makes Christians fully appreciate the sacrifice Jesus made for them.
- The sacrifice of Jesus, God's son, made it possible for Christians to be forgiven for their sins (see page 14).

Why the resurrection of Jesus is important to Christians

- Only God has the power to rise from the dead, so this shows Christians that Jesus was God's Son.
- As Jesus rose from the dead and sits at the right hand of God, Christians believe he is present in the world today, and always.
- Jesus's resurrection shows that sin can be conquered and gives all Christians the hope that there is life after death.

Activities

4   Draw a spider diagram to show why the birth, death and resurrection of Jesus are important for Christians.

5   Explain why belief in Jesus as God's Son is important in the Christian faith.

For discussion

Jesus was more human than divine. Do you agree? Why?

Summary

- Christians believe Jesus is the Son of God. He was conceived by the power of the Holy Spirit and Mary, his mother, was a virgin. This means Jesus was both God and human.
- Christians believe that Jesus was crucified and suffered so that all people could have the chance to be saved from sin and go to Heaven.
- The Resurrection showed that Jesus had conquered sin and death, proving him to be the Son of God.

1.5 The Holy Spirit

Learning outcomes

By the end of this lesson you should be able to:

- describe the meaning of term 'the Holy Spirit'
- give your own opinion, with reasons, about the Holy Spirit
- explain why the belief in the Holy Spirit is important to Christians
- evaluate the importance of the belief in the Holy Spirit for Christians.

Sacred texts

'*The giving of the Holy Spirit*' (Acts 2:1–13)

The Holy Spirit as part of the Trinity

The Holy Spirit is the third part of the Trinity. All parts of the Trinity are equal as they are all one. When we talk about the third part of the Trinity, this means the order in which they were revealed to the world.

After the resurrection, Jesus promised to stay with his followers. After Jesus ascended to Heaven the Holy Spirit continued to guide and inspire Christians.

For discussion

How can you believe in the Holy Spirit if you cannot see it? What does the painting above show?

The Holy Spirit today

Some Christians believe that the Holy Spirit is received through healing and the ability to speak in tongues (see page 75).

Activities

1   In pairs, imagine you were there when the disciples received the Holy Spirit. One of you is a disciple, the other a reporter for radio. The reporter interviews the disciple to find out exactly what happened. Write the script for the interview,

2   Find out about the work of Jackie Pullinger. How does she believe the Holy Spirit has worked in her life and the life of others?

Jackie Pullinger has written a number of books about her life, including *Chasing the Dragon* and *Crack in the Wall*. You might like to try and find a copy of one of these in your local library.

Go to www.heinemann.co.uk/hotlinks (express code 4240P, link to 'Jackie Pullinger') for further information about Jackie Pullinger and the importance of her Christian faith and the Holy Spirit in her life.

The symbols of the Holy Spirit

These are the different symbols used to help Christians understand what the Holy Spirit is like.

The Holy Spirit brings new life to people, in the same way as a dove descended from Heaven when Jesus was baptised.

The Holy Spirit brings peace, as the returning dove Noah sent from the Ark held an olive branch, showing that the flood had receded and God was once again at peace with the world.

Fire was used to show the presence of God. God spoke to Moses out of a burning bush.

It is a symbol of purification. Metals were placed in a fire to purify them. The Holy Spirit cleanses people of their sins.

We know that wind is there – we can feel it and see its effect on things, but cannot see it. The symbol of wind is therefore used to describe God's power and presence in the world.

Why is the Holy Spirit important for Christians?

Christians believe that the Holy Spirit works to change us and make us better people. The qualities we develop are called Fruits of the Spirit, such as love, kindness, faithfulness and self-control.

The Holy Spirit gives people different gifts. All are different but equal, just as parts of the body each have a certain function, but depend on each other to work effectively.

It is through the Holy Spirit that God is with people today. Christians see the Holy Spirit as the comforter, the guide, the counsellor and the inspirer.

> ### Sacred texts
>
> 'The Holy Spirit described as wind' (John 3:8)
>
> 'The baptism of Jesus' (Luke 3:21–22)
>
> 'The fruits of the Holy Spirit' (Galatians 5:22–23)
>
> 'The different gifts of the Holy Spirit' (1 Corinthians 12:4–11)

For discussion

The Holy Spirit is active in the world today. Do you agree?

ResultsPlus

Top tip!

When you see the word 'Why?' in an exam question, remember to always use the word 'Because …' in your answer! This will help you make sure you give reasons for your answer.

Activities

3   Design a stained glass window for a church on the theme of the Holy Spirit. Now explain, either in writing or to the rest of the group, how your window shows what the Holy Spirit means to Christians.

Challenge

4   What does the term 'Paraclete' mean? How does this relate to the Holy Spirit?

Summary

- The Holy Spirit is the third aspect of the Trinity.
- Christians believe that the Holy Spirit inspired the Bible and continues to inspire, guide and empower Christians today.

1.6 Salvation from sin

Learning outcomes

By the end of this lesson you should be able to:

- describe the meaning of sin and salvation
- give your own opinion, with a reason, about salvation from sin
- explain why the belief about salvation from sin is important to Christians
- evaluate the importance of the beliefs about salvation from sin for Christians.

edexcel ⠿ key terms

Atonement – Reconciliation between God and humanity.

Faith – Firm belief without logical proof.

Repentance – The act of being sorry for wrongdoing and deciding not to do it again.

Salvation – The act of delivering from sin, or saving from evil.

For discussion

Look at the seven words displayed opposite. Explain why each of these is a 'bad' thing – a sin.

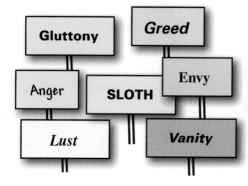

Gluttony · Greed · Anger · SLOTH · Envy · Lust · Vanity

What is a sin?

A sin is an action that breaks God's law. It can be possible for Christians to commit a sin but not break the law of the country, for example, by committing adultery. It is also possible to break the law but not commit a sin, for example, by speaking out against an unjust government.

Christian beliefs about sin

- Sin separates humans from God.
- Original sin is the sin inherited from the actions of Adam and Eve.
- Some Christians believe we are all born with original sin, which is washed away through baptism (see page 63).
- Personal sin is due to a person's own actions – it is a wilful turning away from God.
- For Catholics (see pages 68–69), sins are either mortal or venial. Mortal sins are things like murder, and venial sins are less serious, such as envy.

What is salvation and how is it achieved?

Salvation means being saved from sin. Christians believe that salvation has been made possible through the life, death and resurrection of Jesus. For this reason, Jesus is seen as the saviour of the world. For many Christians, salvation comes through the Church, through receiving the sacraments such as baptism and confirmation. Above all, they believe it is achieved by leading a good Christian life.

For discussion

How is Jesus like Superman? How is Jesus different from Superman?

Activities

1 Think of five words or images to describe what sin means. Then think of five more words or images to describe what salvation means.

The story of Zacchaeus

This story is used to show how salvation can be achieved by having **faith** in Jesus and **repentance** for wrong doings. This then leads to reconciliation, or **atonement** – the repairing of humankind's relationship with God.

Zacchaeus was a tax collector who cheated people out of money.

When Jesus arrived in Jerusalem, Zacchaeus climbed a tree so he could see Jesus over the crowd.

Zacchaeus gave back the money he had cheated from people.

Jesus showed Zacchaeus he had forgiven him.

Why do Christians believe salvation is important?

- If a Christian is saved from sin it means they will have eternal life.
- Jesus's life, death and resurrection were about bringing the possibility of salvation to humankind; therefore it must be what God wants for the world.
- The belief in salvation encourages Christians to do right and behave towards others in a loving way.

Activities

2 Imagine you are Zacchaeus. Write your diary entry for the day you met Jesus.

3 Explain, with examples, what the difference is between forgiveness and reconciliation.

4 Explain why salvation from sin is important for Christians.

What is original sin?

Christians hold different views on what original sin is and how the story of Adam and Eve should be interpreted.

- Some Christians believe that original sin is the sin committed by Adam and Eve when they disobeyed God in the Garden of Eden; it is passed on to future generations. Therefore all humans are born with original sin.
- Other Christians do not believe that Adam and Eve actually existed. They believe it is just a story to explain how people react when faced with a choice between good and bad. For them, original sin means all the bad things that exist in the world and each individual has to make their own choice to turn away from sin.

For discussion

What are the consequences of sin in the world today?

Activities

Challenge

5 For Catholics, sins can be forgiven through the act of confession. Find out more about the sacrament of reconciliation. Do you think all sins should be forgiven?

Go to www.heinemann.co.uk/hotlinks (express code 4240P, link to 'Catholic Encyclopaedia') to find out more about the sacrament of reconciliation.

Summary

- Sin is what separates humans from God.
- Salvation means being saved from sin. This has been made possible through the death and resurrection of Jesus.
- The story of Zacchaeus shows how having faith in Jesus and repenting of sin leads to atonement – reconciliation with God.

1.7 Love of God

Learning outcomes

By the end of this lesson you should be able to:

- describe what love of God means to Christians
- give your own opinion, with reasons, about loving God
- explain how the loving God affects the lives of Christians
- evaluate the importance for Christians of loving God.

What does love mean?

love is...

...a necessity, not a luxury.

For discussion

Think of as many different ways as you can that we use the word love. Then write a text message explaining what love is.

Activities

1 Write an article for a church magazine entitled 'How you can show love of God today'.

2 Interview a Christian to find out what love of God means to them.

Sacred texts

'The Greatest Commandment' (Mark 12:28–34)

'The commandment to love God' (Deuteronomy 6:4–5)

'The commandment to love your neighbour' (Leviticus 19:18)

'God is Love' (1 John 4:7–12)

The Greatest Commandment

When asked which was the greatest of all the commandments, Jesus said there were two that summed up all the laws found in the Jewish Bible (Old Testament). The most important one was to love God with all your heart, and the second was to love others.

This is why Christians believe the most important Christian value is love.

How Christians show their love of God

We show love for people we care about by trying to get to know them better, listening to them and wanting to do things to help them. Christians show their love of God in the same way, by talking to him through prayer, learning more about him through reading the Bible and doing as he asks them to do.

In their daily lives, Christians show this love for God in the following ways:

- going to church to receive Holy Communion
- praying to God regularly
- being baptised and, for many, by being confirmed
- getting married in church and having a Christian funeral
- following the teachings given in the Bible and by the Church
- leading a good Christian life and loving others as God has asked.

For discussion

Do you think it is important for people to love God today?

The importance of love of God for Christians

- The Bible and the Church teach Christians that love of God is fundamental to the Christian faith – from this everything else comes.
- Jesus taught that love of God was the most important of all the commandments.
- It is through loving God that Christians can hope for eternal life with God.
- If Christians love God, then they worship him – this gives them the strength to spread the good news about God and Jesus.
- It is through the love of God that Christians find the inspiration and strength to show their love of others through their deeds and actions – helping to make the world a better place.

For discussion

How can you love God when you cannot see or touch him?

Activities

3 Explain why the love of God is important for Christians.

Challenge

4 In 1 John it says 'God is Love'. What do you think this means?

For discussion

Look at the photograph above. Many Christians visit Walsingham in Norfolk each year on a pilgrimage. They walk the holy mile between the Catholic and Anglican churches. Some people do it barefoot. How does taking part in such a pilgrimage show love of God? Why do you think walking barefoot is a way of showing love for God?

Summary

- Jesus said the most important commandment is to love God.
- Christians show their love of God through worship, prayer and showing love for others.
- The love of God gives Christians the hope of eternal life.
- The love of God both inspires and gives Christians the strength to live a good Christian life.

1.8 Love of others (1)

18

Learning outcomes

By the end of this lesson you should be able to:

- describe the teaching about love of others from the parable of the Good Samaritan
- give your own opinion, with a reason, about the love of others
- explain the meaning and importance of love of others for Christians
- evaluate the importance of love of others for Christians.

edexcel ::: key terms

Compassion – A feeling of pity that makes one want to help the sufferer.

For discussion

Look at the photograph and explain what you think needs to be done to help these children.

The commandment to love others

Jesus taught that to love your neighbour as yourself was the second most important commandment. For Christians, loving your neighbour is an important part of the teachings of Jesus. Neighbours are not just the people who live next door to you, but every other person. There are many ways that you can show love for your neighbour, from helping an elderly person with their shopping, returning a lost wallet or praying for these who are sick.

Jesus told parables that help Christians to understand what love of others means. Two of the best known are 'The Good Samaritan' and 'The Sheep and the Goats'.

Sacred texts

'The Greatest Commandment' (Mark 12:29–31)

'The commandment to love your neighbour' (Leviticus 19:18)

'The parable of the Good Samaritan' (Luke 10:25–37)

For discussion

'Love Changes Everything' is the title of a famous song. Do you think love can change everything? How?

The parable of the Good Samaritan

A parable is a simple story with a deeper meaning. Jesus was asked the question 'Who is my neighbour?' In reply he told this parable.

A Jew was travelling from Jerusalem to Jericho when he was attacked and left for dead by robbers. Two Jewish people, a priest and a Levite (a Jewish person who acted as a minister in the Temple), ignored him and walked past. A Samaritan (a person from a different area who did not get on with the Jews) stopped and helped the man, took him to an inn and paid for him to be looked after.

After he told the parable, Jesus asked the question 'Which of these do you think was a neighbour to the man?'

Activities

1 Design an ideas map to show all the ways Christians can show love of others.

2 In groups, think about how the parable of the Good Samaritan could be given a modern setting. Plan and perform your own modern-day version of the parable.

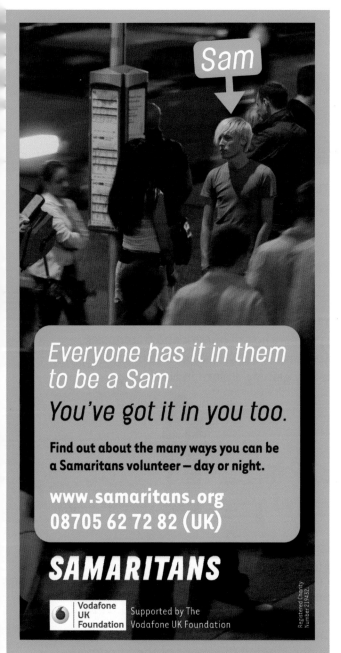

The meaning of the parable of the Good Samaritan

The people listening to the story would have expected the Jewish religious leaders (the Levite) to help their fellow Jew as they would have known the commandment to love others from the Jewish Scriptures. But for them this did not involve action to help others. They did not show **compassion** for the injured man as the Samaritan did.

In this parable, Jesus is making the following points about loving others:

- People's needs take precedence over everything else. The priest and Levite were probably too busy or preoccupied with their religious and daily lives to involve themselves with the injured man.
- Showing compassion ignores any religious, social or cultural divides. The Samaritans were considered outsiders by the Jews and would have nothing to do with them. It would have shocked the people that a Samaritan was the one who shows compassion for the injured man.
- Love is a very practical thing; it involves action. The Samaritan went beyond just stopping; he also provided for the man's needs by paying for his keep at the inn.
- Being a follower of Jesus means being involved in practical help – at the end of the parable Jesus says 'Go and do likewise'.

Activities

3 Imagine you have been asked to preach in your local church on the meaning of the parable of the Good Samaritan. Write your speech.

4 'We should show compassion to people in the UK first.' Do you agree?

Challenge

5 Saint Francis said 'Preach the Gospel at all times and when necessary use words.' What do you think he meant by this?

For discussion

What do the modern 'Samaritans' do? Why do you think this name was chosen?

To find out more about the Samaritans, go to www.heinemann.co.uk/hotlinks (express code 4240P, link to 'Samaritans'). You will find lots of useful information, including pictures, interviews and video clips, about the organisation and what its members do.

Summary

- Jesus said that loving your neighbour is the second part of the Greatest Commandment.
- The parable of the Good Samaritan teaches Christians that everyone is their neighbour and that love involves practical action.

1.9 Love of others (2)

Learning outcomes

By the end of this lesson you should be able to:

- describe the teaching about love of others from the parable of the Sheep and the Goats
- give your own opinion, with a reason, about the love of others
- explain the meaning and importance of love of others for Christians
- evaluate the importance of love of others for Christians.

Sacred texts

'*The parable of the Sheep and the Goats*' (Matthew 25:31–46)

The parable of the Sheep and the Goats

In this parable Jesus explained how people will be judged at the end of the world by the Son of Man (a title given to Jesus) and how it will be decided who will go to Heaven.

In this parable Jesus shows that loving others means caring for people who are hungry and thirsty, sick, poor or in prison. Those who show love of others will be rewarded by gaining a place in Heaven.

Jesus is described as a shepherd who is separating the sheep from the goats.

The sheep are the good people who fed the hungry, gave shelter and clothes to the needy, looked after the sick and visited those in prison. The goats are the people who ignored the needs of the hungry, homeless, sick and those in prison.

For discussion

'It is impossible for Christians to show love to everyone. Do you agree?

For discussion

Look at the photograph. Who is person? Find out how she showed love of others in her life and work.

Activities

1 Prepare a PowerPoint® presentation or a storyboard that tells the story of the parable of the Sheep and the Goats.

Love of others leads to a better world for all

You have to show love of others to get into Heaven

The importance of love for others

It is the second part of the Greatest Commandment

Many of Jesus's teachings show the importance of loving your neighbour

The importance of Jesus's teachings about love of others

For discussion

Look at the photograph. Should a Christian give money to such a person? Give reasons for your answer. Think carefully about the arguments for and against.

'You cannot love your neighbour without loving God.' Do you agree?

The meaning of the parable of the Sheep and the Goats

Jesus said that everyone should treat others as they would treat Jesus himself. Jesus said whenever they did something for others in need, it was as if they were doing it for Jesus himself.

Throughout this parable Jesus shows his humanity by identifying himself with those in need and those who are suffering.

It is through people's actions, in the way they show love for others, that they will be judged. Those who fail to show compassion will not be saved or go to Heaven.

Activities

2 Find out about one person or an organisation that has followed the teachings of Jesus given in the parables of the Good Samaritan or the Sheep and the Goats.

Activities

3 From your own experience, describe a situation where you have seen love for others in action.

4 Explain what the parable of the Sheep and the Goats teaches Christians about the love of others.

Challenge

5 In 1 Corinthians Chapter 13, Paul explains the meaning of Christian love. Make a list of all the qualities he mentions. Which do you think are the three most important? Explain why.

Summary

- The parable of the Sheep and the Goats teaches Christians that those who show love for others through their actions will be rewarded by going to Heaven.
- Love of others is the second part of the Greatest Commandment – Christians believe this will help to make a better world for all people.
- The parable of the Sheep and the Goats reminds Christians of the humanity of Jesus and that he knows and shares our pain and suffering.

1.10 How religious communities express their love of God

Learning outcomes

By the end of this lesson you should be able to:

- give your own opinion, with reasons, about how the love of God is expressed at Taizé
- explain how the love of God is expressed at Taizé
- evaluate the importance of love of God as expressed through a religious community such as Taizé.

The Taizé community

Taizé is a village in central France that is home to a community of monks. The monks are drawn from both the Catholic and Protestant traditions (see pages 92–93) and from many countries across the world. Each year, tens of thousands of young people, aged 17–30, visit the community to share in its way of life. Time for worship, prayer and reflection are at the heart of the Taizé experience.

How Taizé began

The community was started by Brother Roger in 1940. During and after the Second World War he helped many refugees. Many were Jews escaping from Germany. In 1949 Brother Roger founded a religious community. The rules for the community included:

- celibacy (see page 52)
- the sharing of material goods
- obedience
- silence at meals.

Today, the community is self-supporting. Welcoming others to help them explore their Christian faith is an essential part of Taizé life.

For discussion

- Look carefully at the poster and list all the activities you think take place at Taizé.
- How do you think the love of God is expressed at Taizé?

Activities

1 Imagine you are a young Christian visiting Taizé for the first time. Write a letter home describing what you do and your thoughts and feelings about your stay.

Daily life at Taizé

Monday to Friday

8.15 am	Morning prayer, then breakfast
10.00 am	Introduction to the day and quiet reflection or small group discussion
12.20 pm	Midday prayer, then lunch
2.00 pm	Optional song practice

During the afternoon international small groups or work to support the community

5.15 pm	Tea
5.45 pm	Theme workshops
7.00 pm	Supper
8.30 pm	Evening prayer, with songs in the church, followed by night silence.

Thoughts about Taizé

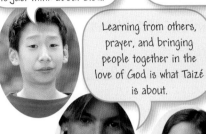

> The luxuries in life are stripped away allowing you to just think about God.

> Time at Taizé allowed me to think about my future and what direction God wanted me to go in.

> Learning from others, prayer, and bringing people together in the love of God is what Taizé is about.

> After my stay at Taizé I now feel ready to energise my local church.

Worship at Taizé

Taizé has developed its own distinctive style of singing used in worship. Short songs, repeated again and again help people to focus on the meaning of the words. It can become almost a form of meditation.

Prayer follows the monastic tradition and the community gathers for prayers three times a day. The services at Taizé are often candlelit and include hymns, psalms, scripture readings and prayers.

For discussion

Look at the photographs and thoughts about Taizé. How can a visit to Taizé help a Christian today?

Activities

2 **Role play** In pairs, imagine one of you has just been to Taizé and the other thinks that the money spent on the trip would have been better used by giving it to a charity. Write down what you say in your conversation.

3 Explain how the love of God is shown through a religious community.

Activities

Challenge

4 When Pope John Paul II visited Taizé he said: 'Like you… the Pope is only passing through. But one passes through Taizé as one passes close to a spring of water. The traveller stops, quenches his thirst and continues on his way.'

What do you think he meant by this?

How the love of God is shown through the life at Taizé

The monks have dedicated their lives to God and to serving others by helping them to explore and strengthen their faith.

Many young Christians make a pilgrimage each year to spend time in prayer and study to show their love of God. A simple lifestyle is adopted by all; prayer and communion with God are central to the daily routine.

The music and style of worship used expresses the love of God and has helped many Christians who haven't been to Taizé to share in this.

Visit the Taizé website at www.heinemann.co.uk/hotlinks (express code 4240P, link to 'Taizé') to find out more about the life of the monks and the experience of visitors.

For discussion

'Love of God is best expressed through good deeds, not through prayer.'

Summary

- Many young Christians spend time at Taizé to express their love of God.
- Through worship, prayer, study and in their daily life, the monks and visitors to Taizé express their love of God.

1.11 How religious communities express their love of others

24

For discussion

Look at the cartoon. Is this child poor? What does it mean to be poor today?

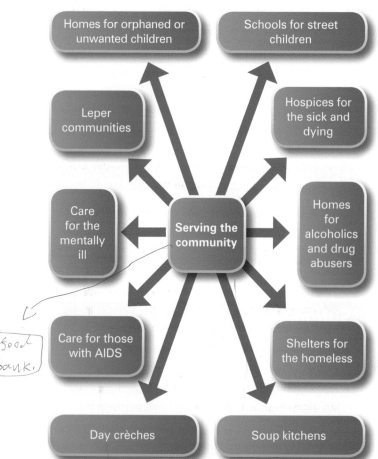

The Missionaries of Charity serving the community

The Missionaries of Charity help sick and abandoned children, the old and dying, lepers and AIDS victims, and the homeless. The sisters work in many different communities from Kolkata to New York and in towns around the UK. How they help will depend on the needs of the community.

Activities

1 Explain how the Missionaries of Charity show love of others.

The Missionaries of Charity

The Missionaries of Charity are a religious community founded by Mother Teresa in 1950 in Kolkata (Calcutta) in India. The aim of the community was to care for those too poor to care for themselves. The Missionaries of Charity have expanded today to consist of over 4,500 nuns who work in more than 100 countries.

The nuns follow the vows of celibacy, poverty and obedience (see page 52) and a fourth vow to give 'Wholehearted and free service to the poorest of the poor'.

'No, I can't afford to buy you those trainers or any chocolate today!'

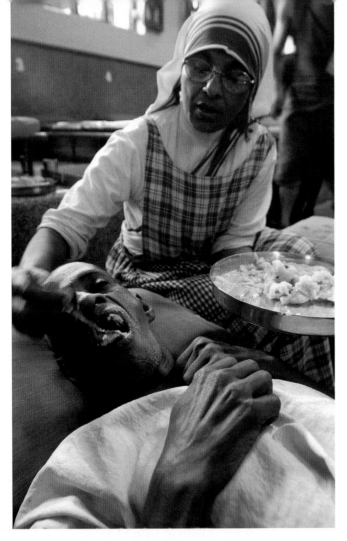

How love of others is expressed through the work of the Missionaries of Charity

- The sisters follow the Christian teaching to love your neighbour, as they are willing to help all those who are in need, whatever their religion or background .
- Real love of others is shown by the sisters, as they are often required 'to love the unlovable' – those in the community who others have rejected.
- They are an active community showing their love of God through serving the poorest of the poor. They are acting like the sheep in the parable of the Sheep and the Goats (see pages 20–21).
- Love of others is often seen in the small things that are done for other people. For those who are dying, the important thing is to show that in their last hours of life someone cares for them.

Activities

4 Find out about the work of the Missionaries of Charity in the UK.

5 In groups, research and prepare a presentation for the rest of the class on another religious community that shows love of others through its life and work.

For discussion

'Loving the unlovable' is the only way to show true Christian love of others. Do you agree?

Summary

- The Missionaries of Charity express their love of others by helping the poorest of the poor in many communities throughout the world today.
- The Missionaries of Charity put the Christian teaching to love your neighbour into practice by helping many different groups of people, many of whom are ignored or rejected by the rest of society.

Activities

2 Imagine you are a journalist doing a story about the work of the Missionaries of Charity. Write a short article to go with this picture.

Challenge

3 This is a prayer Mother Teresa said and shared with others. Why would the Missionaries of Charity continue to find this of help to them?

Lord, make me an instrument of your peace:
where there is hatred let me sow love;
where there is injury, pardon;
where there is doubt, faith;
where there is despair, light;
where there is sadness, joy.
Lord, may I not so much seek to be consoled, as to console;
to be understood, as to understand;
to be loved, as to love.
Because it is in giving that we receive,
in pardoning that we are pardoned.
Amen.

1.12 How a Christian church shows love of God and others in the local area

Learning outcomes

By the end of this lesson you should be able to:

- give your own opinion, with reasons, about how a church shows love of God and others in the local area
- explain how a church shows love of God and others in the local area
- evaluate the importance of how a church shows the love of God and others in the local area.

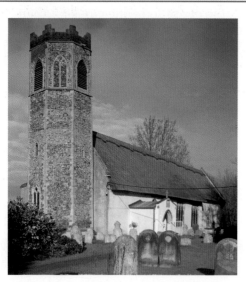

All Saints Church, Buckenham, Norfolk.

For discussion

Many small villages in the UK, like Old Buckenham in Norfolk, have active local churches. Find out the name and location of the churches in your local area.

A church in a local community

A church is the building where Christians gather together to worship God. It is the focal point for most Christians within the community, and many different activities take place within the church or church buildings. The love of God and love of others can be seen through the life of a local church.

How a church shows the love of God through worship

- The church is the centre of worship for Christians. Worship is the way Christians express their love of God.
- Most Christians will regularly attend church services.
- At important times during the Christian year, Christians come together to celebrate events such as Christmas and Easter.
- At key points in their lives, Christians show their love of God through ceremonies (such as baptism and weddings) that take place in the church.

How a church shows the love of others through social activities

The church is a centre for social activities for the local community. Many activities take place there that show love for others as taught by Jesus (see page 55). Here are some examples:

- youth clubs
- mother and toddler groups
- Cubs and Brownies
- lunch clubs for older people
- events to raise money for charities.

Many of these activities are not just open to members of the congregation but are open to all members of the local community.

Activities

1 Find out about the activities that take place in a church in your local area. You could perhaps visit the church, interview a member of the church or carry out some research using the internet (many churches will have their own websites or newsletters). Then decide if and how you think each of the activities show love of God, love of others, or both.

The church as a spiritual centre for Christians

The church is a centre of education and inspiration for many Christians, which helps them to grow and develop in their love of God. The local church is usually led by someone who has studied that faith in depth and may have taken holy orders (see pages 96–97). Local Christians can seek advice and support from them on matters of faith.

The church provides many opportunities for Christians to explore and show their love of God through discussion and study. A lot of churches have Bible study groups, Sunday school for children, prayer groups and classes for those about to be confirmed or baptised.

For discussion

- Is a church more than just a meeting place?
- Why do you think many churches run Fairtrade stalls?

The church as a place of social concern

One of the ways Christians can show their love of God is by loving others, as God has asked. This is why many churches are involved in supporting the local community through a wide variety of activities, and encourage their members to be actively involved in social and moral issues that affect the world today.

Many members of local churches are involved in such issues as environmental concerns and world poverty. The inspiration for their action comes from Christian teaching. The church supports them by encouraging their wish to live according to the teachings of Jesus.

Activities

2 Find out about the work of a group such as Church Action on Poverty or Target Earth. Why do you think a church would choose to support such a group?

3 Find out how a church in your local community helps individual Christians to love God.

4 Find out which charities /organisations the church in your local area supports. Why have they chosen to support these particular charities?

Challenge

5 The church is a place of salvation. What do you think this means? (see pages 40–41)

For discussion

The most important thing a Christian church can do is to show love of others. Do you agree?

Summary

- A local church shows the love of God through being the focal point for worship and study of the Christian faith.
- The members of a church show their love of others through concern for those in their local community and in the wider world.

examzone

Know Zone
Section 1: Beliefs and values

Quick quiz

1 Name the three aspects of the Trinity.

2 Name two creeds.

3 What is the incarnation?

4 Name three symbols of the Holy Spirit.

5 What is salvation?

6 What is meant by atonement?

7 What is the Greatest Commandment?

8 Name three ways in which Christians show love of God.

9 Name two of the parables told by Jesus that help Christians understand what love of others means.

10 State three ways in which a local church can show love for others.

Plenary activities

1 Design an ideas map to summarise all the key Christian beliefs.

2 Divide a piece of paper into two halves. On one side write the heading 'Love of God', and on the other side 'Love of others'. Now record all you know about each one on the relevant side.

Find out more

- For more information about Christianity compiled by the BBC, go to www.heinemann.co.uk/hotlinks (express code 4240P, link to 'BBC Christianity').

- The New Lion Handbook called *Christian Belief* is a useful and detailed reference book (The New Lion Handbook *Christian Belief*, edited by Alister McGrath, ISBN 978 0 745 95157 7).

- Parish magazines can give you a good insight into the beliefs, values and activities of local Christians. Copies can usually be found (often free of charge) in the local parish church or community centres.

- Look out for television programmes such as the BBC series *The Big Questions* and documentaries that explore Christian beliefs, values, history, customs and traditions. Easter and Christmas are a good time to look out for these. Programmes about church buildings are also shown quite frequently. Try searching the BBC iPlayer for any suitable programmes that may have been screened recently.

- Films such as *Bruce Almighty* and *The Lion, the Witch and the Wardrobe* and even some episodes of *The Simpsons* explore Christian themes, beliefs and values.

Student tips

- Don't confuse 'the Greatest Commandment' with 'the Golden Rule'.

- Remember that Christians believe God is One and that he is experienced through the three aspects of the Trinity.

- Remember some Christians believe in the 'big bang' theory and evolution and think that this is the way God created the universe.

- Make sure you can explain what the parables of the Good Samaritan and the Sheep and the Goats teach Christians about love of others.

- Remember to name the religious communities and local church you have studied when answering exam questions.

Self-evaluation checklist

Read through the following list and evaluate how well you know and understand each of the topics.

How well have you understood the topics in this section? In the first column of the table below use the following code to rate your understanding:

Green – I understand this fully

Orange – I am confident I can answer most questions on this

Red – I need to do a lot more work on this topic.

In the second and third columns you need to think about:

- Whether you have an opinion on this topic and could give reasons for that opinion if asked
- Whether you can give the opinion of someone who disagrees with you and give reasons for this alternative opinion.

Content covered	My understanding is red/orange/green	Can I give my opinion?	Can I give an alternative opinion?
The meaning and importance for Christians of believing in God as Unity, Trinity, Father and Creator.			
The meaning and importance for Christians of believing Jesus is the Son of God.			
The meaning and importance for Christians of believing in the Holy Spirit.			
The meaning and importance of Christian beliefs about salvation from sin.			
The meaning and importance of loving God and how it affects Christians' lives.			
The meaning and importance of Christian teachings on the love of others.			
How the love of God and others is expressed in the life of a religious community.			
How a Christian church shows the love of God and others.			

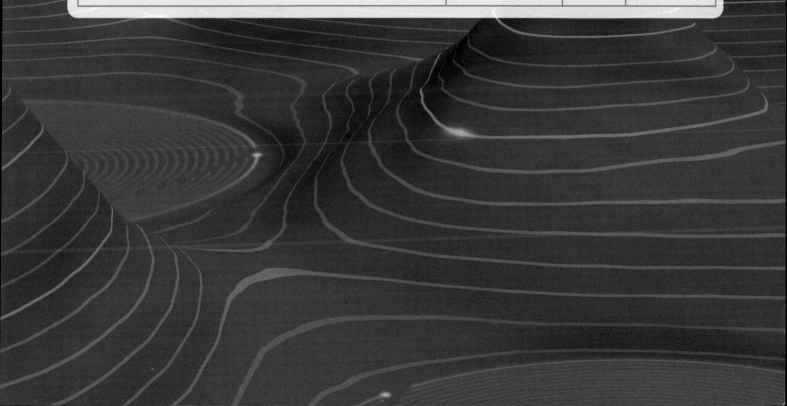

Know Zone
Section 1: Beliefs and values

In your exam you will be given a choice of two questions on this section. Each question will include four tasks (a)–(d), which test your knowledge, understanding and evaluation of the material covered.

- A 2-mark question will ask you to define a term.

- A 4-mark question will ask your opinion on a point of view.

- An 8-mark question will ask you to explain a particular belief or idea.

- A 6-mark question will ask for your opinion on a point of view and ask you to consider an alternative point of view.

There is no need to write in full sentences. A phrase and/or examples are all that are required.

'Explain why' means you need to give reasons why the belief is important. It is a good idea to use the word because in your answer.

Mini Exam Paper

(a) What is **faith**? (2 marks)

(b) Should people believe in the Virgin Birth? (4 marks)

Give **two** reasons for your point of view

(c) Explain why believing in God as the Father is important for Christians. (8 marks)

(d) 'It does not matter if you sin as long as you say sorry to God.'

In your answer you should refer to Christianity.

(i) Do you agree? Give reasons for your opinion. (3 marks)

(ii) Give reason why some people might disagree. (3 marks)

You just need to give two clear reasons for your point of view. You do not have to give another view point.

You need to decide whether you agree. Then give three brief reasons or you could give more detailed ones but be sure not to repeat yourself. Then give an alternative view point in the same way.

ResultsPlus
Watch out!

Even if you write a very good explanation, you can lose marks if you fail to read and answer the question fully. For example, how many reasons did the question ask for; were you asked to refer specifically to Christianity?

Remember that all (d)-type questions ask for your opinion, but they also ask you to give the opposite point of view with reasons. If you don't, you may only score half marks!

Support activities

1 Look at these two (b)-type questions.

- Do you think it is important for people to love God?

- Should God be described as Father?

Each question will ask you to give reasons for your opinion. Practise using these two questions. Write a list of your reasons for agreeing or disagreeing.

ResultsPlus
Maximise your marks

(c) Explain why believing in God as the Father is important for Christians. (8 marks)

Student answer	Examiner comments	Build a better answer
Belief in God the Father is important because he is the Creator of the world. He made the world we live in and created us like a Father. God the Father gave his son to save us, which shows he loves us just as a father does... We ask God to forgive us. Without this you would not get salvation and go to Heaven. We go to Heaven to be with God the Father.	In this answer the candidate gives two reasons; God is the Creator so he is like a Father and God the Father sending Jesus to show His fatherly love. The rest of the answer does not answer the question. If the candidate had linked the idea of a father as a person who forgives they would have developed the second reason.	Belief in God the Father is important because he is the Creator of the world. He made the world we live in and created us like a Father. God the Father gave his son to save us, which shows he loves us just as a father does. We ask God to forgive us. As he is seen as our Father he will forgive us so we can achieve salvation and go to Heaven. In the Lord's Prayer Jesus taught us to call God Father. Belief in God as a loving caring Father must be important for Christians because Jesus said this is what we should call him and he was God's son.

Community and tradition

Introduction

In this section you will explore, think and learn about the meaning of the Christian community and tradition. You will consider the meaning and importance of the Bible and the Church for different groups of Christians. You will also look at topics such as the importance of the Virgin Mary for Christians, and celibacy of the clergy.

Learning outcomes for this section

By the end of this section, you should be able to:

- give definitions of the key terms and use them in answer to GCSE questions
- describe the different Christian views on the authority of the Bible and the Church
- describe the role of the Pope, the local priest or minster and the local church within the Christian community
- explain why the Bible is important and has authority for Christians, and the different views about the authority of the Church
- explain the different Christian attitudes towards the Virgin Mary and the celibacy of the clergy
- express your own point of view about the Bible, the authority of the Church and the Pope, the Virgin Mary and the celibacy of the clergy, giving your reasons
- evaluate points of view about community and tradition within the different Christian traditions, showing you have thought about different views from your own, giving reasons and evidence.

In this section you will learn:

- why some Christians believe the Bible is the direct word of God and why others believe it was written by humans about their experience of God
- why the Bible has authority and importance for Christians
- the meaning and importance for Christians of the Church being the means to faith and salvation
- the meaning of the apostolic tradition and succession and their importance for the Roman Catholic Church
- the meaning of Protestant beliefs about the authority of the Church and their importance for Protestant Christians
- why Christians have different attitudes to the role and importance of the Virgin Mary
- the role and importance of the Pope and bishops in the Roman Catholic Church
- the role of the priest or minister in the local church
- why Christians have different attitudes to the celibacy of the clergy
- the role and importance of the church in its local area.

edexcel ⚌ key terms

Anglican Churches	celibacy	Old Testament
apostolic	laity	ordination
bishops	New Testament	Orthodox Churches
catholic	Nonconformist Churches	papacy

Fascinating fact

The Bible has been translated into 2,018 languages. In comparison, Shakespeare has only been translated into 50 languages.

1   How does the story of Coventry Cathedral help you to understand the idea of tradition?

2   In the old part of the cathedral the altar was constructed from the rubble of the old cathedral and the cross was made from its charred beams.

   Why do you think the Christian community chose to do this?

3   Many Christians from all over the world visit the cathedral each year. Why do you think they do that?

4   The stained-glass windows and the tapestries in the cathedral are often admired. Find out more about them. Why do you think they were chosen to go into the new cathedral?

5   To take a virtual tour of the cathedral, go to www.heinemann.co.uk/ hotlinks (express code 4240P, link to 'Coventry Cathedral virtual tour').

Coventry Cathedral has been a place of worship for over 900 years. The new cathedral was consecrated in 1962. It was built next to the ruins of the old cathedral that was destroyed by bombs during the Second World War.

2.1 The Bible as the word of God

Learning outcomes

By the end of this lesson you should be able to:

- describe the meaning of Old Testament and New Testament
- give your own opinion, with a reason, about the Bible as the direct word of God
- explain why some Christians believe the Bible is the direct word of God
- evaluate the belief that the Bible is the direct word of God.

edexcel ⠿ key terms

New Testament – The second part of the Bible, which records the life of Jesus and the early Church.

Old Testament – The first part of the Bible, which Christians believe foretells Jesus.

Activities

1 Compile a factfile about the Bible.

The Bible

The Bible is the holy book for Christians. It contains 66 different books divided into the **Old Testament** and **New Testament**. The Old Testament has 39 books, which contain God's laws that were given to the Jewish people. These books also tell the history of the Jewish people and include prophecies about the coming of Jesus. In the New Testament are the four Gospels, The Acts of the Apostles (the first followers of Jesus) and letters from the early Christian leaders. From the books of the New Testament, Christians can learn about the life and teachings of Jesus and about the early Christian Church.

The Bible as the direct word of God

Some Christians believe that what is written in the Bible came directly from God. This means that they believe God used human beings to record his words. Therefore, some Christians believe that what is written in the Bible must be true, as it was not written by humans but came from God. These Christians believe that what the Bible says is the absolute truth, and that any contradictions found in it can be explained. This view is sometimes called 'fundamentalist'.

For discussion

Do you think the Bible is the direct word of God? Give the reason for your answer.

A page from the Lindisfarne Gospels showing the first page of Matthew's Gospel. What does the picture above tell us about what Christians think about the Bible?

The fundamentalist view of the Bible

Many people argue that the Bible cannot be the direct word of God because it contains contradictions for the modern world. Fundamentalists say that these issues can be explained. They believe that if what the Bible says is different from the modern scientific point of view, then science must be wrong. For example, in Genesis it says that God created the world in six days – therefore, if the Bible says this, then it must be what happened.

Fundamentalists believe that the Bible, as the word of God, is the only true guide to life and should be followed exactly as it is written. The commandment to keep the Sabbath holy means that fundamentalists do not work or take part in any activities on a Sunday, in order to keep the day special.

Activities

2 **(a)** Find out what Martin Luther or John Calvin believed about the Bible.

   (b) Find out what part the Bible played in the Reformation of the Church in Europe in the 16th century.

3 Design an ideas map to show why some Christians believe the Bible is the direct word of God.

Challenge

4 Find out about the Scopes Trial that took place in the USA in 1925. What different views of the Bible were taken by the people involved in the trial?

You can read more about the Scopes Trial by following the online links for this topic. Go to www.heinemann.co.uk/hotlinks (express code 4240P, link to 'Scopes Trial 1' and 'Scopes Trial 2').

For discussion

The film *Chariots of Fire* tells the story of Eric Liddell. He ran in the 1924 Olympic Games and won a medal, but he never took part in his best event – the 100 metres. Find out why.

Why some Christians believe the Bible is the direct word of God

- Even though the Bible was written over a period of about 1,300 years and by many different people, there is a unity in the message, showing there must be one author behind it – and that author must be God.
- Jesus himself refers to the Jewish scriptures, now the Old Testament, as 'the Word of God'.
- The prophecies of the Old Testament were fulfilled through the life and death of Jesus, showing the Bible to be the true word of God.
- Through personal religious experience, some Christians believe the Bible has come directly from God.

Summary

- Some Christians believe the Bible came directly from God and that what it says is the absolute truth.
- Some Christians believe that the Bible came from God as there is a unity in the message.
- Fundamentalists believe that the Bible cannot be wrong.

2.2 The inspiration for the Bible

Learning outcomes

By the end of this lesson you should be able to:

- give your own opinion, with reasons, about the belief that the Bible was written by humans inspired by the Holy Spirit
- explain why some Christians believe the Bible was written by humans, rather than by God
- evaluate the belief that the Bible was written by humans about their experiences of God.

For discussion

Why do you think the painting opposite is called *The Inspiration of St Matthew*?

The Bible inspired by the Holy Spirit

All Christians believe that God speaks to them through the words of the Bible, but Christians hold different views on how this happens. Some Christians believe the writers of the Bible were inspired by the power of the Holy Spirit (see pages 12–13). They believe that the personality of the individual writers can be seen in what they wrote, and that they were influenced by their own time and culture when writing about their experiences.

The Bible written by humans about their experiences of God

Other Christians think the writers of the Bible were just ordinary human beings writing about their experiences of God. Just like many authors, they were inspired to write and to share their insights and views on human life. These writers are thought to have great insights about God and are able to help others understand what God is like and what he wants for humans.

For some Christians, the Bible was inspired by God, but experienced, interpreted and written by ordinary human beings.

For discussion

Do you think the Bible is the word of God or humans?

Activities

1 Draw a diagram or picture that summarises the two different views about how the Bible was inspired by God.

Why some Christians believe the Bible was inspired by the Holy Spirit

The view that the Bible was inspired by the Holy Spirit is often referred to as 'conservative'. This comes from the word 'conserve', which means to protect. Some Christians hold this view because:

- The Bible is a book about faith. It was not intended as a science or history book, and therefore it is spiritually true but not literally true.
- There are key truths that were inspired by the Holy Spirit – for example, that Jesus died for all human sins and rose again. These beliefs need to be protected and accepted.
- They are not concerned about contradictions in the Bible. They accept that the writers are just giving different versions of the same story. The important thing is the overall meaning and message, and not the detail.

Why some Christians believe the Bible was written by humans

The view that the Bible was written by humans who wanted to share their experiences of God is often called the 'liberal' view. The Bible is seen as just a book to guide Christians in their lives today. Christians hold this view because:

- The writers were writing about their own times; therefore, they reflected their understanding of the world at that time, which is not the same as the world today.
- The writers were influenced by the accepted beliefs of their own time, but Christianity has moved on since then. For example, some Christians have come to accept that men and women are equal, which is different from the view found in the teachings of the early Christian Church.
- Many of the passages in the Bible attempt to explain important truths and are to be understood symbolically and not literally.

Activities

2   In pairs, one takes on the role of a conservative Christian and the other the role of a liberal Christian. Explain to each other what you believe about the Bible.

Challenge

3   Read Ephesians 5:22–24. Think about how a fundamentalist, a conservative and a liberal Christian would interpret this passage.

Summary

- Some Christians believe that the Bible was written by humans but was inspired by the power of the Holy Spirit.
- Other Christians believe that the Bible was written by humans who were inspired by God to write about their own experiences and views.
- For many Christians the Bible is a spiritual book and is to be understood symbolically not literally.

For discussion

How might different Christians understand the story of the feeding of the five thousand (Matthew 14:15–21)?

2.3 The authority of the Bible

Learning outcomes

By the end of this lesson you should be able to:

- give your own opinion, with reasons, about the authority of the Bible
- explain why the Bible has authority and importance for Christians
- evaluate why the Bible has authority and importance for Christians.

The Bible today

For most Christians today, the Bible has authority because it is believed to be the word of God speaking to humankind. This means that what it teaches is important and should be believed and followed. The Bible is used in a variety of different ways by Christians:

Prayer

When Christians pray or want to get closer to God they use passages from the Bible to help them.

Teaching

The Bible is used to help Christians understand and explore their faith.

As a guide

The teachings in the Bible help Christians make important decisions in their lives.

Activities

1 In pairs, make a list of when and how a Christian might use the Bible. Now share your list with another pair and add in any examples you missed.

2 Explain why the Bible is important for Christians.

3 Design and carry out a survey to find out what people today think about the Bible.

For discussion

Look at the photograph above. What do you think is happening here? What does this tell you about the role of the Bible in society today?

Why the Bible is important for Christians

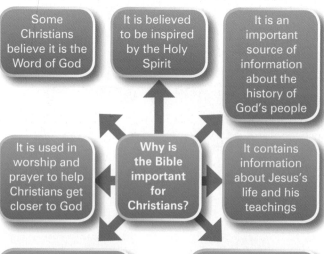

Some Christians believe it is the Word of God

It is believed to be inspired by the Holy Spirit

It is an important source of information about the history of God's people

It is used in worship and prayer to help Christians get closer to God

Why is the Bible important for Christians?

It contains information about Jesus's life and his teachings

It is a guide for how to live a good Christian life

It contains the teachings of the first Christian leaders, such as St Paul

For discussion

Do you think the Bible is important today? Why?

Different attitudes to the authority of the Bible

All Christians would agree that the Bible has authority, but different views are held about its importance.

- For Christians who believe that it is the direct Word of God, the Bible has absolute authority as the Word of God cannot be wrong.
- For Christians who believe it was inspired by the Holy Spirit, the Bible has absolute authority in matters of belief, but on matters of science and on some moral issues they believe it needs to be reinterpreted for the world we live in today.
- For Christians who believe the Bible was written by humans about their experience of God, it has authority, but the conscience of individual Christians can have an equal role to play.

Activities

Challenge

4 Gideons International is an organisation that is dedicated to the distribution of the Bible to people throughout the world. Find out more about their work and why they do it.

- Go to www.heinemann.co.uk/hotlinks (express code 4240P, link to 'Gideons') where you can find out more information about Gideons International and their work to help you with the activity.
- Go to www.heinemann.co.uk/hotlinks (express code 4240P, link to 'Bible Society') to find out more about the Bible and what different people think about it.

 ResultsPlus
Build Better Answers

Do you think the Bible is important today? Give **two** reasons for your point of view. (4 marks)

■ **Basic, 1-mark answer**
Gives a personal response with one brief reason.

● **Good, 2-mark answer**
Gives a personal response with either two brief reasons or one developed reason.

▲ **Excellent, 4-mark answer**
Gives a personal response with two developed reasons.

For discussion

Christians base their belief that abortion is wrong on the commandment 'Do not murder' (Exodus 20:13). Think of some other modern-day issues and then find an appropriate Bible teaching that would help a Christian decide what to believe or do about that issue.

Summary

- The importance of the Bible can be seen in the way Christians use it to help them to worship and come closer to God.
- The Bible is important to all Christians as it contains the life and teaching of Jesus and the history of the early Church.
- All Christians believe that the Bible has authority, but different views are held on how it should be interpreted.

2.4 The Church as the means to faith and salvation

Learning outcomes

By the end of this lesson you should be able to:

- describe the meaning of the Church as the means to faith and salvation
- give your own opinion, with reasons, about the Church as the means to faith and salvation
- explain the importance for Christians of the Church as the means to faith and salvation
- evaluate the importance for Christians of the Church as the means to faith and salvation.

edexcel key terms

Laity – All the people of the Church who are not chosen to be bishops, priests or deacons.

Ordination – Making someone a priest by the sacrament of holy orders.

For discussion

In 1859 Charles Blondin became famous for being the first person to cross a tightrope over the Niagara Falls. Each time he went across he performed a different feat – crossing on stilts, on a bicycle, and blindfold while pushing a wheelbarrow. When he asked if anyone would sit in the wheelbarrow, no one would. Later his manager agreed to be carried on Blondin's back. What do we learn about faith from this story?

The Church

The Church means everyone who belongs to the Christian Church. This includes the **laity** and all those who have been through the process of **ordination**. Jesus chose twelve disciples to continue his work on Earth. This movement soon grew into the Christian Church. Today, there are many different forms of Christianity, but all have their roots in the early Church. It is through the Church today that Christians learn about their faith.

The Church as a means to faith

All Christians see the Church as teaching and supporting the Christian faith. During services the Christian message is taught and explained. Classes are often run before people undertake ceremonies such as confirmation or marriage. Sunday schools and Bible study groups are often run by churches each week.

The Church as a means to salvation

Christians believe that salvation has been made possible through the life, death and resurrection of Jesus. This is the foundation of the Christian Church. For many Christians, salvation is achieved by being a member of the Church (see pages 14–15) and through the sacraments of baptism and confirmation, received through the Church (see pages 62–67).

For discussion

Do you think the Church is the only way to God?

Catholic teaching about the Church as the means to faith and salvation

Catholic Christians believe that the Church keeps alive the true faith that was handed down to the disciples from Jesus and passed on to the bishops. This is known as the apostolic succession (see page 43). The Church is the guardian of the true faith and interprets it for Christians today. Therefore, the Church is the one source of faith, as it preserves the Christian message as taught by Jesus.

For discussion

Look at the photograph. Describe what is happening in this picture. What do you understand by the term salvation?

Catholic Christians believe that only the Pope and the bishops (see pages 48–49) can interpret the Bible and the tradition of the Church, as they are guided by God. Therefore, they are the ones who have authority to pass on the Christian faith.

It is through receiving the body and blood of Christ during the Mass that Jesus comes into people's daily lives, making salvation possible (see pages 14–15).

Activities

1 Write a short text message summarising what you understand by the phrase 'The Church is the means to faith and salvation'.

Activities

2 For Protestant Christians the Bible itself and the individual's personal response to the teachings of Jesus are the main means to faith and salvation. Why do you think this is?

3 Explain why Catholic Christians believe the Church is the means to faith and salvation.

4 The Church is also referred to as the Body of Christ. Find out why Christians describe it in this way.

FRENCH ARABIC PORTUGUESE

Sacred texts

'The Church as the Body of Christ' (1 Corinthians 12:12–13)

Summary

- Christians believe that the Church is the means to faith, as it is through the Church that people can learn and believe the message of Christianity.

- Catholic Christians believe that as part of the Church you will receive salvation.

- For members of the Catholic Church, salvation is made possible through the sacraments of baptism, confirmation, the act of confession and the Mass.

2.5 Apostolic tradition and succession

42

Learning outcomes

By the end of this lesson you should be able to:

- describe the meaning of apostolic tradition and succession
- give your own opinion, with a reason, about apostolic tradition and succession
- explain the importance for Catholic Christians of the apostolic tradition and succession
- evaluate the importance for Christians of the apostolic tradition and succession.

For discussion

Who were the apostles? How many of them can you name?

Activities

1 Draw a diagram to show what you understand by the apostolic tradition.

edexcel ⠿ key terms

Apostolic – The belief that the Church is founded on the apostles who were appointed by Jesus.

Bishops – Specially chosen priests who are responsible for all the churches in a diocese.

Catholic – Universal or worldwide.

The apostles and the early Church

The apostles are the twelve disciples chosen by Jesus. They knew Jesus, and were witnesses to his life and teachings. Jesus gave them the authority to start the Church. They passed on the message Jesus had given them to the first Christians.

Peter was the leader of the apostles and became the first Bishop of Rome – the first Pope. So today the office of Pope can be traced back directly to the apostle Peter who was appointed by Jesus.

The apostolic tradition

The apostles were instructed by Jesus to pass on the gospel. 'Gospel' means 'good news' and it took two forms.

The written gospel

This includes the four Gospels found in the New Testament (see page 34), written by Matthew, Mark, Luke and John. It can also refer to all the New Testament writings. All these books are found in the Bible today.

The oral gospel

After Jesus's death, the apostles passed on to the **bishops** of the early Church the teachings given by Jesus. These teachings became part of the tradition of the Church.

Tradition and the Bible are the two main sources of authority for the Catholic Church.

For discussion

Why is it important for Catholic Christians that the office of Pope can be traced back to St Peter?

What is apostolic succession?

The **apostolic** succession is the belief that the Pope and the bishops continue in the world today the mission Jesus gave to Peter and the apostles. Catholic Christians believe that the Holy Spirit (see pages 12–13) continues to guide and inspire the Pope and bishops today.

The Nicene Creed

The Nicene Creed is the statement of beliefs used by Christians. It says 'We believe in one, holy, **catholic** and apostolic Church.' Christians believe the Church is apostolic because:

- it was founded on the apostles whom Jesus appointed
- the bishops received the message from the apostles and it continues to be passed on
- St Peter was the first Pope and his authority has been passed on to all other Popes.

The importance of the apostolic tradition and succession

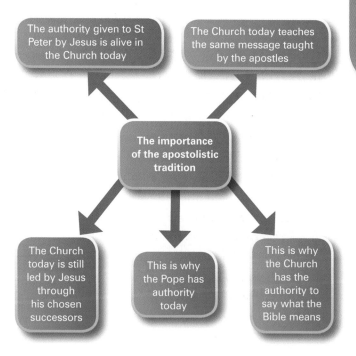

The authority given to St Peter by Jesus is alive in the Church today

The Church today teaches the same message taught by the apostles

The importance of the apostolistic tradition

The Church today is still led by Jesus through his chosen successors

This is why the Pope has authority today

This is why the Church has the authority to say what the Bible means

43

For discussion

- This is a statue of St Peter. Why do you think he is shown holding the keys to Heaven?
- For Catholic Christians the Church should be the only source of authority. Do you agree?

Activities

Look at Article 9 of the Roman Catholic Catechism to find out what it says about the apostolic role of the Church. Go to www.heinemann.co.uk/hotlinks (express code 4240P, link to 'Catechism') to find the information you need.

2 Explain what is meant by apostolic tradition and succession.

3 Produce four PowerPoint® slides to explain why the apostolic succession is important for Catholic Christians.

Summary

- The Church is apostolic because it was founded on the apostles, the followers of Jesus.
- Apostolic succession means that the Pope and bishops continue the tradition passed on to the apostles by Jesus.
- The authority of the Church and the Pope comes directly from the apostles and is the link between Jesus and the world today.

2.6 The authority of the Church for Protestant Christians

44

Learning outcomes

By the end of this lesson you should be able to:

- understand what is meant by Anglican Churches, Nonconformist Churches and Orthodox Churches
- give your own opinion, with a reason, about the authority of the Church for Protestant Christians
- explain the importance of Protestant beliefs about the authority of the Church
- evaluate the importance of Protestant beliefs about the authority of the Church.

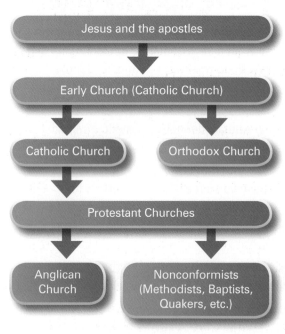

Activities

1 In pairs, think of a way that helps you remember the key terms in this section.

2 Write a summary of the important events in the development of the Christian Church.

edexcel ⠿ key terms

Anglican Churches – Churches that are in communion with the Church of England.

Nonconformist Churches – Protestant Churches separated from the Church of England (e.g. Methodist).

Orthodox Churches – National Churches that are in union with the Patriarch of Constantinople (e.g. the Russian Orthodox Church).

A brief history of the Church

Up until the year 1054 there was just one Church – the Catholic Church. The Pope led the Church from Rome. The Church was very strong in Eastern Europe, in those countries we know today as Greece, Russia and Turkey. There was a big disagreement about whether the Pope should be the leader of the whole Christian Church. Because of this, there was a split in the Church – the Western Church became the Catholic Church and the Eastern Church became the **Orthodox Church**.

In Western Europe, including Britain, the main religion was Catholic Christianity, with the Pope in Rome as its leader. In the early 1500s some people became unhappy about the state of the Catholic Church. They thought it needed reforming as it had lost its way, and had become more interested in its own power and importance than in the message of the Bible. The result was a split in the Catholic Church, and the beginning of the Protestant Churches.

Protestants today

There are many different Protestant Churches today. The **Anglican Church** has many different Churches worldwide but the parent Church is the Church of England. The Church of England was formed by Henry VIII after he had a disagreement with the Pope, who would not allow him to have a divorce. So Henry broke with Rome, no longer accepting the authority of the Pope, and made himself the Head of the Church of England.

Some Protestants did not feel that the religious reforms had gone far enough. They wanted the laity to have a bigger role in the Church, and for more importance to be given to the teaching found in the Bible. Many **Nonconformist Churches** were established, including the Methodists, Baptists, Quakers and the Salvation Army.

The Church guides and advises

Most Nonconformist Churches do not have priests or bishops. They have 'ministers' who guide and advise but who have no authority to tell people what to believe or how to behave. Knowing God and learning about faith comes through reading the Bible, through prayer and applying one's conscience to all matters.

For discussion

What authority do Members of Parliament (MPs) have? Why do you think people are elected as MPs? How is it different from the monarchy?

Authority within the Church of England

- In the Church of England the Church has authority because its followers believe in the Apostolic Church, as stated in the Nicene Creed.
- The Church of England has a hierarchy of leadership, with the Archbishop of Canterbury at the head. He is seen as a spiritual leader. His authority comes from the fact that people know him to have knowledge of religious matters.
- The General Synod is an elected group of people within the Church of England who discuss and agree matters of belief and moral issues. They are a representative group of the Church, including bishops, priests and laity, and this means that many will accept and follow their guidance.

For discussion

The General Synod is sometimes called the Christian Parliament. Why? What authority do you think it should have?

Summary

- The Church of England believes in the Apostolic Church so its bishops have authority.
- Members of the Church of England will accept and follow the guidance of the General Synod and the Archbishop of Canterbury.
- Most Nonconformists believe that knowing God and following their faith come through reading the Bible and through prayer, and that the Church is there to support, guide and advise.

2.7 Different Christian attitudes to the Virgin Mary

Learning outcomes

By the end of this lesson you should be able to:

- describe the different attitudes Christians have to the role of the Virgin Mary
- give your own opinion, with reasons, about the role and importance of the Virgin Mary
- explain why Christians have different attitudes to the role and importance of the Virgin Mary
- evaluate the role and importance of the Virgin Mary within Christianity.

Activities

1 Make a list of the qualities you think a perfect mother would have. Place them in order of importance. Now explain to someone else why you chose the top three.

2 Explain why Mary is called (a) the Virgin Mary and (b) the Mother of God.

Sacred texts

'The role of Mary is foretold' (Isaiah 7:14)

'The Angel visits Mary' (Luke 1:26–38)

'Mary at the crucifixion' (John 19:25–27)

Mary, the Mother of Jesus

Christians believe that Mary was the mother of Jesus and for that reason has an important place within Christianity. Mary is often referred to as the Virgin Mary, as she did not conceive the baby Jesus in the normal way by having sexual relations with Joseph. Jesus was therefore God's Son, and not Joseph's.

In Luke's Gospel an angel visits Mary and tells her she will have a child, showing she was chosen by God to be the mother of Jesus. Mary is often called the Mother of God.

Mary as a role model for Christians

All Christians view Mary as a role model for them today because:

- Mary was completely devoted to God. She followed his plan without questioning him or her beliefs
- throughout Jesus's life Mary showed her love for him, and when he was dying on the cross she was one of the few to remain with him
- throughout her life Mary showed the personal qualities of obedience, trust, faith, courage, love and putting God first in her life.

For discussion

- Choose five words that best describe the picture above. What do you think this picture tells you about the role of the Virgin Mary in Christianity?
- Roman Catholic Christians often refer to Mary as 'Our Lady'. Discuss what you think they mean by this title.

The grotto at Lourdes in France.

For discussion

Look at the photograph. Find out why Catholic Christians make a pilgrimage to visit this place.

Go to www.heinemann.co.uk/hotlinks (express code 4240P, link to 'Lourdes') for the the link to the official website for Lourdes (which includes images and videos, as well as a webcam where you can see what is happening at the shrine 24 hours a day).

The Virgin Mary in the Catholic Church

The Virgin Mary is given a special place in the Catholic Church. She is seen as the link between Heaven and Earth because she was the Mother of Jesus. Catholics do not worship Mary but ask her to intercede with Jesus on their behalf. Therefore, Catholic churches will have a statue of Mary and often a Lady Chapel dedicated to her. They use the 'Hail Mary' as a special prayer.

ResultsPlus
Watch out!

Some candidates confuse the Virgin Birth (of Jesus) with the Immaculate Conception (of Mary).

There are special feasts in the Catholic Church that show how important Mary is. Two examples are:

- *the Immaculate Conception*: Mary is believed to have been conceived without receiving original sin (see page 15) so she would be worthy of giving birth to Jesus.
- *the Assumption*: upon her death Mary was 'assumed' up to Heaven, body and soul. In Heaven, Mary is able to pray for Christians on Earth.

The place of Mary in the Protestant Church

For Protestants, Mary has a special place as the mother of Jesus. Mary is seen as an ordinary human who is an example of a life dedicated to God. The creeds state that Jesus was born to the Virgin Mary so this is also a fundamental belief of the Church.

Most Protestants, however, do not accept such beliefs as the Immaculate Conception and the Assumption, as they are not recorded in the Bible – they are teachings of the Catholic Church.

Activities

3 Explain why the Virgin Mary is important for Catholic Christians.

4 Why do you think Catholic Christians refer to Mary as the Mother of the Church?

Summary

- All Christians believe that Mary is important as she was the mother of Jesus and acts as a role model for them today.
- Catholics believe the Virgin Mary has a special place as she was born without sin and is in Heaven, so can intercede on their behalf.

2.8 The Pope and bishops in the Catholic Church

Learning outcomes

By the end of this lesson you should be able to:

● describe the role of the Pope and bishops in the Catholic Church

● give your own opinion, with a reason, about the role and importance of the Pope and bishops

● explain the role and importance of the Pope and bishops in the Catholic Church

● evaluate the role and importance of the Pope and bishops in the Catholic Church.

edexcel ▦ key terms

Papacy – The office of the Pope.

For discussion

'All Catholics should do as the Pope says.'
Do you agree?

The papacy

The Pope is the ultimate authority in the Catholic Church. His authority can be traced back to Peter whom Jesus appointed to be the founder of the Church. This is known as apostolic succession (see page 43). The Pope is also known as the Bishop of Rome. He is seen as the head of the worldwide Catholic Church. Each Pope is elected by the cardinals, who are guided by the Holy Spirit. He remains as Pope until his death.

Bishops

A bishop is a priest who the Pope chooses to be responsible for the churches in a diocese. He is in charge of all the priests in his diocese; he ordains, appoints and disciplines them. He acts as a link between the local parishes and the Church in Rome. Bishops are responsible for ensuring that the Catholics in the diocese follow the teachings of the Church.

Pope Benedict XVI in Rome at Easter.

For discussion

Look at the photograph above. Why do you think there are so many people there?

Activities

1 Draw a diagram to show the hierarchy in the Catholic Church.

2 Find out which diocese you live in, who is the bishop for your diocese, and who is the cardinal for England and Wales.

To find out more about the role of a bishop within the Catholic Church, go to www.heinemann.co.uk/hotlinks (express code 4240P, link to 'Bishop').

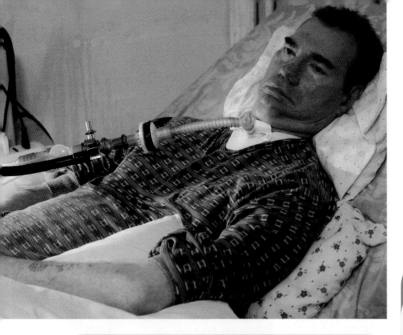

The authority of the Pope today

The Pope is seen as the spiritual leader of the Church. He has special authority to ensure that the teachings of Jesus are preserved and proclaimed throughout the world. This authority comes from the Pope being the successor to St Peter. As he is responsible for the Magisterium, the Pope is responsible for preserving and defining the Catholic faith.

Activities

3 Imagine you have been invited to give a talk about the role and importance of the Pope. Prepare a PowerPoint® presentation to accompany your talk.

4 Explain why the Magisterium is important for Catholics.

Challenge

5 The Pope is known by a number of different titles. Find out why each one is used, and what it means.

- Supreme Pontiff of the Universal Church
- Sovereign of the State of the Vatican
- Vicar of Jesus Christ
- Supreme Pastor

Find out more about the role and importance of the Pope by going to www.heinemann.co.uk/hotlinks (express code 4240P) and link to 'Importance of the Pope'.

For discussion

In Italy in 2006 Piergiorgio Welby, who was terminally ill, wanted euthanasia legalised so that he would be allowed to die. The role of the Catholic Church is to advise Christians how they should respond to such issues. What other modern-day issues do you think Catholics would need advice on? Why do you think Catholics do not use the Bible as the only source of authority?

The Magisterium

The Pope leads the Council of Bishops in interpreting the Bible and apostolic tradition for Catholics today. Their interpretation is seen as the living teaching of the Church and is known as the Magisterium. It gives teachings on moral issues and defines the beliefs of the Catholic Church.

The teachings of the Magisterium are either found in the Catechism or 'encyclicals' – official letters from the Pope.

The Magisterium is important for Catholics because:

- it updates and interprets Catholic teachings in response to modern-day issues
- it makes sure that the key beliefs of the Church are not changed
- Catholics throughout the world follow its teachings, so ensuring unity among the Church worldwide
- it gives clear guidelines on how to live a good life so that salvation is possible.

For discussion

'The Church does not need bishops.' Do you agree?

Summary

- Catholics believe the Pope is important as he is the successor of St Peter and therefore has special authority.
- It is the role of the Pope and bishops to interpret the Bible and apostolic tradition for Catholics today through the Magisterium.

2.9 The role of the priest or minister in a local church

50

A Church of England priest

A Church of England priest, often referred to as a vicar, is the religious leader for a parish. They spend a number of years studying and training for the role before they are finally ordained by the bishop. They now have the authority to minister to the laity.

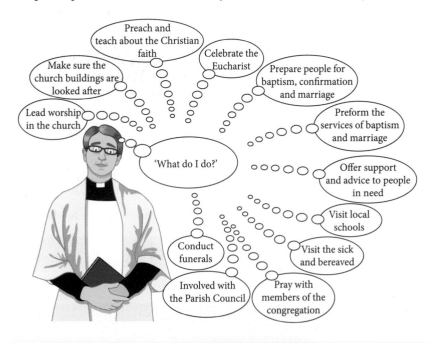

The Vicar of Dibley *is a popular comedy series about the life and work of a Church of England woman priest. Make a list of the things a vicar/priest does. You might find watching an episode helpful.*

Go to www.heinemann.co.uk/hotlinks (express code 4240P, link to 'Day in the life of a vicar/pastor') where you will find a section on a day in the life of an Anglican vicar and a Baptist pastor.

Activities

1 Imagine you are a vicar; write a 'blog' about a typical day in your life.

2 In small groups, imagine you are on a committee that has been asked to select your next vicar. Design an advert for the job. Write a job description and personal specification. Prepare the interview questions.

For discussion

Do you think women make good priests? Give reasons for your answer.

Why do you think that as part of the ordination service the priests lie flat on the ground?

The parish priest in the Catholic Church

A Catholic parish priest is responsible for administering the sacraments of Eucharist, baptism (see pages 62–63), marriage, reconciliation and anointing the sick. The sacraments are the foundation of the Catholic Church so the priest's role is vital.

- The priest hears the people's confessions and has the authority to forgive them for their sins by giving them a penance to perform to show that they are sorry.
- When people are seriously ill the priest will carry out the sacrament of anointing the sick. It gives strength to the sick or helps prepare them for death.
- The priest represents Christ at the Mass and it is the priest who blesses the bread and wine. A Catholic is required to attend Mass each week and without the priest this would not be possible.

- The priest is the link between the bishop and the parishioners, so he is responsible for ensuring that the teachings of the Church are carried out in his parish.
- Like the Church of England vicar, the Catholic parish priest carries out many different roles that help, support and educate the people in his parish.

Activities

3 Interview a local priest, vicar or pastor to find out how they see their role in their church. Write a report of your findings.

Challenge

4 Baptists believe in the authority of the Bible. For Baptists, all people who believe in Jesus as the Saviour can be in direct personal contact with God. Therefore, there is no need for a priest to act on their behalf. The Baptist pastor is chosen by the church congregation to guide and lead its members.

Make a list of all the things you think are involved in the role of a Baptist pastor. How is their role similar to and different from that of a Catholic priest?

For discussion

'A priest is the most important person in the Church.' Do you agree?

Summary

- The main roles of a priest are to lead worship in the church, and to guide, advise and support the members of the church.
- A Catholic priest is important because he represents Jesus at the Mass and has the authority to release people from their sins.

2.10 Celibacy of the clergy

Learning outcomes

By the end of this lesson you should be able to:

- describe the different Christian attitudes to the celibacy of the clergy
- give your own opinion, with a reason, about celibacy of the clergy
- explain why Christians have different attitudes about celibacy of the clergy
- evaluate the different attitudes to the celibacy of the clergy.

edexcel ⋮⋮⋮ key terms

Celibacy – Living without engaging in any sexual activity.

Activities

1 In pairs, agree two advantages and two disadvantages of the clergy being celibate.
2 Outline the different attitudes to celibacy of the clergy.

What do you think are the advantages and disadvantages of a priest being married?

The Catholic view

The Catholic Church requires priests and bishops to be **celibate** and not to marry. Married men can become deacons – people who are called to assist the priests in caring for the community. The Church believes that husbands and wives have responsibilities to love and care for each other and their children. Therefore, a married priest cannot give his life to the service of others as he is required to do.

The Orthodox view

The Orthodox Church requires bishops to be celibate, but not priests. They think that a bishop has too many responsibilities to be married.

Other Christian Churches

No other Churches require bishops, priests or minsters to be celibate and they are allowed to marry. Some may, however, choose to be celibate to help them to dedicate their lives to the service of God.

ResultsPlus
Top tip!

To give a _developed_ reason for your viewpoint, give more detail and/or an example to explain your point of view.

Why are Catholic priests celibate?

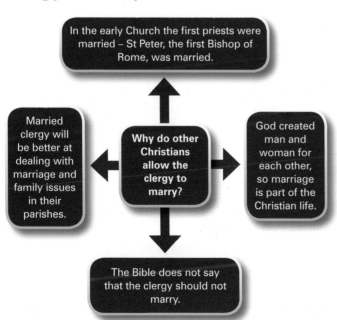

St Paul recommended celibacy as the best way of living.

Jesus was not married – he devoted his life to preaching about the Kingdom of God and serving others. Priests today follow his example.

It means that the priest is not distracted by his own family matters and can give his full attention to the people in his parish.

Why are Catholic priests celibate?

As the priest represents Jesus at the Mass, therefore he must be like him – male and celibate.

It has been Church law for nearly a thousand years and the papacy has made it clear that it is opposed to the idea of priests being married.

It allows priests to be completely dedicated to the service of God and to follow their vocation (see page 92).

Why do other Christians allow the clergy to marry?

In the early Church the first priests were married – St Peter, the first Bishop of Rome, was married.

Married clergy will be better at dealing with marriage and family issues in their parishes.

Why do other Christians allow the clergy to marry?

God created man and woman for each other, so marriage is part of the Christian life.

The Bible does not say that the clergy should not marry.

Activities

3 Look at the following newspaper clipping. How would you answer the question it raises?

> ### Ireland is running out of priests
>
> The Catholic Church in Ireland faces a crisis. In the next 20 years the number of priests will have fallen by two thirds. Is the Church's rule on the celibacy of the clergy to blame?

4 Design and complete a table to show the different Christian attitudes to the celibacy of the clergy.

Challenge

5 Monks and nuns take a vow of chastity. Find out more about this vow. How does this help you to understand why Catholic priests are celibate?

Sacred texts

'Jesus' teaching on marriage and divorce' (Mark 10:6–10)

'St Paul recommends celibacy as the best way of living' (1 Corinthians 7:32–35)

For discussion

Should all priests be celibate?

Summary

- Catholic priests are required to be celibate so they can dedicate their whole lives to the service of God, the Church and others.
- All other Christians allow their priests to marry, but the Orthodox Church requires bishops to be celibate.

2.11 The role and importance of a church in its local area

54

Learning outcomes

By the end of this lesson you should be able to:

- give your own opinion, with a reason, about the role of a church
- explain the role and importance of a church in its local area
- evaluate the importance of a church in its local area.

Activities

1 Make a list of the events and activities you thought of that take place in a church. Rank them in order of how important you think they are to the local Christian community.

2 Visit your local parish church, or speak to a representative of the church, to find out about all the activities that go on there on a daily, weekly and annual basis.

For discussion

The photograph above shows a church Sunday school. Name as many different events, ceremonies and activities as you can that take place in a parish church.

ResultsPlus
Watch out!

Many candidates confuse the 'church' as a building with the 'Church' (with a capital' C'), which refers to the whole Christian community.

The parish church

The Church (with a capital C) means the whole Christian community and a church (with a small c) means a place of worship. The main purpose of a local parish church is to be a witness to God and the life of Jesus in the local community. Its three main roles are:

- as a centre for worship where the Eucharist, baptism, confirmation, weddings and funerals take place
- as a place where Christians can come together to share and grow in their faith. This helps to develop a sense of belonging to the local and worldwide Christian community
- a social centre that ensures all members of the community are cared for.

For discussion

Should the church be at the heart of the local community?

The importance of the church in the local community

- For many Christians salvation is made possible through the Eucharist, baptism and confirmation and it is at the church that these are received (see page 41).
- It gives Christians opportunities to grow and strengthen their faith. Many churches have Bible groups which help people to discuss and learn more about their faith.
- The church helps to develop a sense of belonging to the Christian community. It is a place where Christians can come together to share their faith and receive support from each other.
- It is a place Christians can go to find both spiritual and social support. The priest or minister is there to give advice and guidance.
- The church is a way of ensuring the Christian community grows, and the message of Jesus is brought to more people. Many churches run Sunday schools and youth groups where children can learn more about the Christian faith.
- The church is important for many people because it provides help and support for different members of the community. Groups for mothers and toddlers, lunch clubs for the elderly and youth clubs are run by local churches. This helps to develop a sense of community in a local area.

St Martin-in-the-Fields, London.

For discussion

- Look at the photograph of St Martin-in-the-Fields, in central London. It does a lot of work to help the homeless in the city. Why do you think it does this work?
- Churches have no role to play in the local community today.' Do you agree?

The church in the community

Many churches have become important centres for giving help and support to their local community. Some city-centre churches will provide services for the homeless, such as soup kitchens. Many local churches provide a social service to the local community, and will help people whether they are members of the church or not.

Activities

Challenge

3 With the changing nature of family life in the United Kingdom, there are now more single parents as well as children being brought up by step-parents. What role do you think the local parish church can have in supporting family life?

Activities

4 Collect or draw five pictures or images that show the importance of a church to a local community. Explain why you chose each one.

Summary

- The church is important as a centre for worship. It is a place where the Eucharist, festivals and such events as baptisms and marriages are celebrated.
- The church gives people a sense of belonging to the local and worldwide Christian community.
- The church as a social centre offers support and care for all members of the local community, whether or not they are members of the church.

examzone

Know Zone
Section 2:
Community and tradition

Quick quiz

1 Name two books found in the New Testament.

2 Give two reasons why the Bible is important for Christians.

3 Who are the laity?

4 Who was the first bishop of Rome?

5 What does the Nicene Creed say about the Church?

6 Name two Nonconformist Churches.

7 What is the General Synod?

8 State two Roman Catholic beliefs about the Virgin Mary.

9 What is the name of the current Pope?

10 Name four things a parish priest is expected to do.

Plenary activities

1 Design an ideas map to show different Christian beliefs about the Bible.

2 Hold a class debate on the role of the Church for Christians today.

3 In pairs, write your own 'quick quiz' questions for this section. Then swap them with another pair and each pair should then try to answer the questions they have been given. You can mark them!

Student tip

• Remember – not all Christians believe the same thing about the Bible.

• The twelve disciples of Jesus are often called the 'apostles'. This will help you remember what 'apostolic' means.

• The word 'catholic' can be used in two different ways. It is used to refer to a group of Christians often called 'Roman Catholics'. It can also be used to describe the Christian Church as being universal or worldwide.

• Remember – there are many different groups of Christians, so avoid using the word 'all' when you are talking or writing about Christians.

• Don't forget that in the UK the most the popular form of Protestant Christianity is the Church of England.

Self-evaluation checklist

Read through the following list and evaluate how well you know and understand each of the topics.
How well have you understood the topics in this section? In the first column of the table below use the following code to rate your understanding:

Green – I understand this fully

Orange – I am confident I can answer most questions on this

Red – I need to do a lot more work on this topic.

In the second and third columns you need to think about:
- Whether you have an opinion on this topic and could give reasons for that opinion if asked
- Whether you can give the opinion of someone who disagrees with you and give reasons for this alternative opinion.

Content covered	My understanding is red/orange/green	Can I give my opinion?	Can I give an alternative opinion?
Why some Christians believe the Bible is the direct word of God and others believe it was written by humans about their experience of God.			
Why the Bible has authority and importance for Christians.			
The meaning and importance for Christians of the Church being the means to faith and salvation.			
The meaning of the apostolic tradition and succession and their importance for the Roman Catholic Church.			
The meaning of Protestant beliefs about the authority of the Church and their importance for Protestant Christians.			
Why Christians have different attitudes to the role and importance of the Virgin Mary.			
The role and importance of the Pope and bishops in the Roman Catholic Church.			
The role of the priest or minister in the local church.			
Why Christians have different attitudes to the celibacy of the clergy.			
The role and importance of the church in its local area.			

Find out more

- For more information about Christianity compiled by the BBC, go to www.heinemann.co.uk/hotlinks (express code 4240P, link to 'BBC Christianity').
- *The Lion Encyclopaedia of Christianity* by David Self is a helpful resource about the origins of Christianity and the different Christian denominations.
- To access the Catholic Encyclopaedia, which is a detailed resource of information about Catholic beliefs, go to www.heinemann.co.uk/hotlinks (express code 4240P, link to 'Catholic Encyclopaedia').
- Look out for any coverage in the media of areas covered in this section. For example, the Pope's views on issues are often reported and commented on. Television dramas or documentaries often feature, or give an insight into, some of the topics covered.

Results**Plus**
Watch out!

For (c)-type questions, if you just describe you cannot get more than 2 marks. You must give reasons. If you see the word 'why' in the question, make sure you use the word 'because' in your answer.

Read the question carefully to make sure you are answering the question being asked. Highlighting the key terms in the question should help you.

Support activities

1 Look at these two (d)-type questions.

- 'The Bible is the direct word of God.'

  (i) Do you agree? Give reasons for your opinion. (3 marks)

  (ii) Give reason why some people might disagree with you. (3 marks)

- 'The Church does not need bishops.'

  (i) Do you agree? Give reasons for your opinion. (3 marks)

  (ii) Give reason why some people might disagree with you. (3 marks)

Each question will ask you to give reasons for your opinion and to give reasons why some people would disagree with you.

Practise using these two questions. Write a list of reasons for agreeing and add reasons for disagreeing.

Results**Plus**
Maximise your marks

(a) What is the **New Testament**? (2 marks)

Student answer	Examiner comments	Build a better answer
The story of Jesus's life.	This is a partially correct answer, but it does not mention anything about the early Church.	The second part of the Bible that records the life of Jesus and the early Church.

(c) Should all priests be celibate?

Give **two** reasons for your point of view. (4 marks)

Student answer	Examiner comments	Build a better answer
I think they should as Jesus was celibate and priests follow his example. It allows priests to be completely devoted to God.	The candidate has given two brief reasons why they think priests should be celibate: priests are following Jesus's example and it allows them to devote their life to God.	I think they should because Jesus was celibate and priests follow his example. When celebrating the Eucharist the priest is supposed to represent Jesus, and so should be celibate like Jesus. Also, it allows priests to be completely devoted to God. As they do not have the distractions of a wife and family, they can serve the parish better.

To be awarded the top mark in each level you have to make good use of English. The examiner will be looking for the following:

- a clear and well-planned answer
- use of specialist vocabulary
- very few spelling errors
- use of sentences and paragraphs.

You will get full marks if you give the definition given in the key term glossary at the back of this book (as it appears in the specification).

Mini Exam Paper

(a) What is the **New Testament**? (2 marks)

(b) Should all priests be celibate? Give **two** reasons for your point of view. (4 marks)

(c) Explain why the Virgin Mary is important for many Christians. (8 marks)

(d) 'Everyone should follow the teachings of the Church.'

(i) Do you agree? Give reasons for your opinion. (3 marks)

(ii) Give reasons why some people might disagree with you. (3 marks)

An easy way to get full marks is to give four brief reasons.

You should either agree or disagree with the statement. Don't give a reason for and against as you can only get a maximum of 2 marks.

This part of the question always asks you to respond to a statement. The first thing you have to do is decide if you agree or disagree. Make it clear in your answer to part (i) whether you agree or disagree.

Worship and celebration

Introduction

In this section you will explore, think and learn about how people become members of the Christian Church, and how they worship and celebrate festivals. You will make a study of different churches and discover why different church buildings have certain features.

Learning outcomes for this section

By the end of this section, you should be able to:

- give definitions of the key terms and use them in answer to GCSE questions
- describe key areas of worship and celebration for Christians
- explain why worship and celebration are important for Christians
- express your own point of view about Christian worship and celebration, giving your reasons
- evaluate points of view about Christian worship and celebration, showing that you have thought about different views from your own, giving reasons and evidence
- explain the meaning and importance for Christians of infant and adult baptism and confirmation
- explain the meaning and importance for Christians of the Mass or Eucharist
- explain the meaning and importance for Christians of Christmas, Lent, Holy Week and Easter
- explain why Catholic churches and Nonconformist churches have certain features.

edexcel ⠿ key terms

Advent	confirmation	Mass
believers' baptism	Eucharist	non-liturgical worship
charismatic worship	Holy Week	real presence
commemoration	Lent	transubstantiation

Fascinating fact

Ten per cent of the adult population in the UK go to church at least once a week. That's over six million people!

1 Look at the photograph. Describe what you see.
2 Place small pieces of paper on where you would like to find yourself in the crowd.
  For each one:
  • explain what is going on
  • explain why it is happening
  • describe how it feels being there.
3 How is this similar to worship? How is this different to worship?

3.1 Infant baptism

Learning outcomes

By the end of this lesson, you should be able to:

● describe the meaning of infant baptism

● give your own opinion, with a reason, on infant baptism

● explain why infant baptism is important to many Christians

● evaluate different points of view about infant baptism.

What happens in an infant baptism service?

Many Christians are baptised as babies; the Anglican, Catholic and Orthodox Churches practise infant baptism. The parents and godparents make promises on behalf of the child during the service.

The main features of an Anglican baptism service

● Baptisms usually take place as part of Sunday worship when most people within the church are gathered together.

● The priest welcomes the family of the child who is to be baptised and a thanksgiving prayer is said for the child.

● The parents and godparents are asked a series of questions, which they reply to, e.g., 'Do you turn to Christ as Saviour?' … 'I turn to Christ.'

● The priest makes a sign of the cross on the forehead of the child and invites the parents and godparents to do the same.

● Around the font prayers over the water are said and the congregation profess their faith.

● The priest pours water over the child's head three times, saying 'I baptise you in the name of the Father, the Son and Holy Spirit' (see pages 12–13).

● The priest addresses those present to remind them of their duty to help and support the child in its faith.

● At the end of the service the parents are given a lighted candle for the child.

For discussion

Describe to another person what is happening in the picture above.

Activities

1 Imagine the picture of the baptism on this page is part of a PowerPoint® presentation. Write the script to go with it, describing and explaining what is taking place.

Symbols used in baptism

The pouring of water represents the washing away of sin (see page 14), making the child clean and pure. Water is a symbol of life, starting a new life with God.

Making the sign of the cross is like an invisible badge to show that all Christians are united in Christ and each child belongs to God.

The lit candle shows that Jesus is the Light of the World, guiding the child through life.

Often the child is dressed in a white robe. White is a symbol of purity and new life in Christ.

When signing the cross, perfumed oil, called chrism, can be used as a visible sign of the outpouring of the Holy Spirit.

Why infant baptism is important for many Christians

- Baptism welcomes the child into the Christian Community. During the baptism service the parents promise to provide a Christian upbringing. Both parents and the godparents will encourage the child to make their own commitment to God at the confirmation service.
- Baptism cleanses the child of original sin (see page 15). The baptismal service is seen as a sign of the Holy Spirit entering the life of the child.
- Infant baptism has long been a tradition of the Christian Church.
- Baptism follows the example of Jesus as he was baptised.

For discussion

- How do we know the picture on the left is of the baptism of Jesus?
- Only babies of parents who attend church regularly should be baptised? Do you agree?

Activities

5 Find out what the seven sacraments are in the Catholic Church.

6 Explain why baptism is a sacrament.

Challenge

7 Create your own prayer or blessing that you think summarises the main beliefs about infant baptism that could be used as part of the baptism service.

Activities

2 Explain the symbolism used in an infant baptism service.

3 How can godparents support and encourage a Christian upbringing?

4 Imagine you are a priest. Which two reasons would you use to persuade parents to have their child baptised? Why? What reasons might the parents give for not wanting their child baptised?

Summary

- Baptism welcomes the child into the Christian community.
- During the baptism, parents and godparents promise to provide a Christian upbringing.
- The water of baptism symbolises the child having their sins washed away.
- Baptism follows the example of Jesus who was baptised.

3.2 Believers' baptism

Learning outcomes

By the end of this lesson you should be able to:

- describe the meaning of believers' baptism
- give your own opinion, with a reason, on believers' baptism
- explain why believers' baptism is important to some Christians
- give a reasoned argument why only adults should be baptised.

edexcel ⠿ key terms

Believers' baptism – The baptism of people who are old enough to understand the sacrament.

Claire's baptism

Once I had decided to be baptised I went through a period of preparation. The minister made sure I was fully aware of the commitment I was about to make. On the day of my baptism, I put on my new white clothes to show that I intended to start a new life in Christ. The minister gave a sermon explaining how baptism is an outward sign of belief in Christ. Then he called me forward with the other people who were going to be baptised. The minister asked each of us in turn if we repented of our sins and if we had faith in Jesus Christ. Then I chose to give my testimony, I explained why I wanted to baptised. Then one by one we went down the steps of the baptistery. As I stood in the water the minister said, 'Claire, because you have repented of your sins and have requested baptism. I now baptise you in the name of the Father, and of the Son, and of the Holy Spirit. Amen.' I was fully immersed under the water. Joy of joys, as I arose out of the water I heard the congregation singing my favourite hymn. My sponsor was waiting for me with a towel as I climbed out of the pool. I really did feel God's presence as I entered the water and I know that the Holy Spirit will now guide me through life.

Claire, aged 16

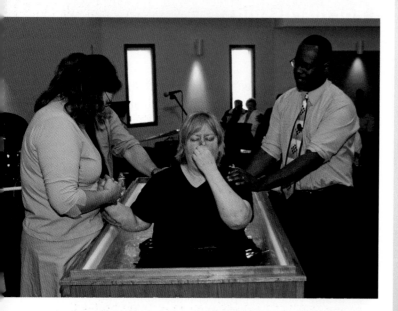

For discussion

Look at the photograph. Think of five words to summarise what is happening.

What is believers' baptism?

Believers' baptism is practised by a number of Churches including the Baptist and Pentecostal Churches. Those who are baptised are old enough to make the decision for themselves. The person being baptised is totally immersed in the water. The service may take place in a pool inside the church, called a baptistery. Sometimes baptism takes place in a river, the sea or a swimming pool.

Activities

1 Create a diagram to show the main stages of the believers' baptism service.

2 In groups, choose part of the service and create a living picture to present to the rest of the group. Be prepared to say what you are thinking when asked.

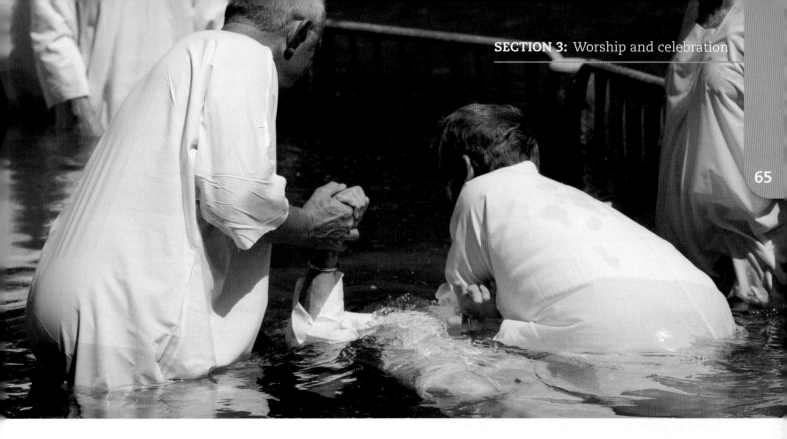

Why believers' baptism is important for many Christians

- Jesus set an example. He was baptised by John the Baptist when he was an adult.
- Jesus commands his disciples to go out and baptise in the name of the Father and the Son and Holy Spirit.
- The early Church practised baptism. On the day of Pentecost, Peter told the people to repent and be baptised.
- It shows the person identifies with the death and resurrection of Jesus. The immersion is a sign that their old life has died and as they leave the pool they have risen to a new life in Christ.
- It is a sign of cleansing. The water is a symbol of God washing away sin.
- It is a public way of declaring your faith and intention to live a Christian life.

Activities

3 Make up a table to show the similarities and differences between infant baptism and believers' baptism.

4 Explain the importance of believers' baptism for some Christians.

For discussion

- Why do you think some people choose to be baptised in a river or the sea?
- 'Only adults should be baptised.' Do you agree? Give reasons why people might disagree with you.

Activities

Challenge

5 Imagine you are a Christian about to be baptised; write the testimony you will deliver at baptism. It needs to explain why you want to be baptised.

Summary

- Believers' baptism takes place when the person is old enough to make the decision for themselves.
- The person is totally immersed in water and baptised in the name of the Father, Son and Holy Spirit.
- They believe they are following the example of Jesus and the early Church.

3.3 Confirmation

Learning outcomes

By the end of this lesson you should be able to:

- describe the meaning of confirmation
- give your own opinion, with a reason, on confirmation
- explain why confirmation is important to many Christians
- evaluate different points of view about confirmation.

edexcel ⠿ key terms

Confirmation – The sacrament when people confirm for themselves the promises made for them in infant baptism.

The confirmation service in the Church of England

The flow chart shows what happens when someone wishes to be **confirmed** in the Church of England.

The candidate completes a preparation programme for a number of weeks before being confirmed.

↓

The service starts with prayers and readings related to the giving of the Holy Spirit.

↓

The candidate is asked a series of questions – for example, 'Do you turn to Christ as Saviour?'

↓

The bishop extends his hands towards those who are to be confirmed and prays that the Holy Spirit will guide them.

↓

Each candidate kneels in front of the bishop, who lays his hands on their head saying, 'Confirm, O Lord, your servant with your Holy Spirit.'

HAPPY 18th BIRTHDAY!

For discussion

At what age should you be considered an adult? Why?

Activities

1 In pairs, act out part of the confirmation service. One person takes the part of the bishop, the other the candidate.
2 Outline the main parts of the confirmation service.
3 Write a programme of the things you think candidates for confirmation should study in their confirmation classes.

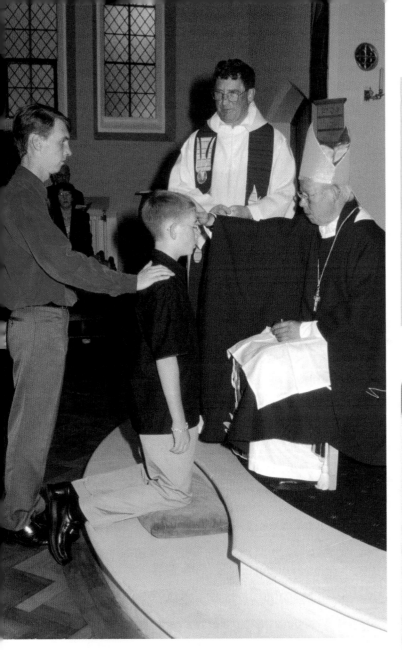

The bishop extends his hands towards those to be confirmed and says:

Almighty and ever-living God,
you have given these your servants new birth in
baptism by water and the Spirit,
and have forgiven them all their sins.
Let your Holy Spirit rest upon them:
the Spirit of wisdom and understanding;
the Spirit of counsel and inward strength;
the Spirit of knowledge and true godliness;
and let their delight be in the fear of the Lord. Amen.

(From *The Book of Common Prayer*)

Activities

4 Research how the Catholic confirmation service might differ from the Church of England service.

5 Find out how you become a member of the Salvation Army.

6 Look into the Quaker views on such services as baptism and confirmation.

You can find out more about both the Salvation Army and the Quakers by going to www.heinemann.co.uk/ hotlinks (express code 4240P, link to 'Salvation Army' or 'Quakers').

Challenge

7 Why might a person who was baptised as a baby choose not to be confirmed?

8 Why are public declarations, such as confirmation services, important for many Christians?

For discussion

- What do you think each person in this photograph is feeling?
- Is confirmation more important than baptism?

Why is confirmation important for many Christians?

- At baptism the vows were made on the child's behalf; now the candidates are taking on that responsibility for themselves.
- It makes the person a full member of the Church.
- It marks the giving of the gift of the Holy Spirit to that person.
- It is a public way of showing your faith and your commitment to being a full member of the Church.

Summary

- At the confirmation service Christians make the promises for themselves that were made for them at their baptism.
- During the service the bishop lays his hands on the candidates as a symbol of giving the gifts of the Holy Spirit to them.
- The candidate is now considered a full member of the Church.

3.4 Catholic Mass

Learning outcomes

By the end of this lesson you should be able to:

● describe the meaning of the Mass

● give your opinion, with reasons, about the Mass

● explain why the Mass is important to Catholics.

edexcel ⋮⋮⋮ key terms

Eucharist – A service celebrating the sacrifice of Jesus using bread and wine.

Mass – The name given to the Eucharistic liturgy of the Roman Catholic Church.

Real presence – The belief that Jesus is present in the bread and wine of the Eucharist.

Transubstantiation – The belief that the bread and wine become the body and blood of Jesus.

For discussion

Look at the photograph. What do the bread and wine represent to Catholics?

What happens during the Mass?

Catholics are expected to celebrate the **Eucharist** every Sunday and on holy days. Catholics refer to it as **Mass**.

Introductory rite	The priest welcomes the congregation.
	The congregation confess their sins and ask for forgiveness.
The Liturgy of the Word	Two readings from the Bible linked to the time of year or the theme of the Mass.
	The congregation respond by reciting psalms.
	A reading from one of the gospels is given by the priest or deacon.
	A sermon is given that focuses on the reading or the special occasion.
	All recite one of the creeds.
The Liturgy of the Eucharist	The bread and wine are brought to the altar.
	Through the Eucharistic Prayers the Last Supper is re-enacted and the bread and wine become the body and blood of Jesus.
	The congregation then come up to the altar, kneel in front of it, and receive the bread and wine. A hymn is sung.
Concluding rite	A final blessing is given to all present.
	The people are dismissed and sent out from the Mass to serve God in the community.

Activities

1 Interview a member of the Catholic Church and find out how they celebrate Mass and what it means to them.

Challenge

2 Create an ideas map to show the importance of the Mass to the individual Catholic, the local community and the Catholic Church.

For discussion

Do you think the Eucharist is the most important form of worship?

Why is the Mass so important for Catholics?

- Catholics believe that the bread and wine actually become the body and blood of Jesus. Jesus is a **real presence** during the Mass.
- The Eucharist is a sacrament. It is through the sacraments that Catholics receive blessings from God and become closer to him.
- By taking part in the Mass, Catholics are obeying the command to 'Do this in remembrance of me.'
- The Mass gives Catholics the spiritual energy to live a Christian life.
- Through remembering the death and resurrection of Jesus at the Mass, Catholics are given the hope of eternal life.
- The Mass unites all Catholics with Jesus and each other.
- Attending Mass on Sunday is a way of observing the commandment, to keep the Sabbath day holy.

What is transubstantiation?

Transubstantiation is the belief that the bread and wine become the body and blood of Jesus.

Why do you think that transubstantiation is referred to as a 'mystery'? Should we believe in something that is a mystery?

ResultsPlus
Build better answers

'Worship is a waste of time.' In your answer you should refer to Christianity.
(i) Do you agree? Give reasons for your opinion. (3 marks)
(ii) Give reasons why some people might disagree with you. (3 marks)

For each of (i) and (ii):

 Basic, 1-mark answers
A simple reason given.

 Good, 2-mark answers
A developed reason or two simple reasons given.

▲ **Excellent, 3-mark answers**
Three simple reasons, two developed reasons or a fully developed reason.
Candidates who do not refer to Christianity in either (i) or (ii) cannot go beyond 3 marks for the whole of the question.

Activities

3 In pairs, put the reasons why the Mass is important for Catholics in rank order, most important first. Now explain your order to another pair.

4 'Going to Mass is the most important thing a Catholic does.' Do you agree? Give reasons for your opinion. Give reasons why some may disagree with you.

Summary

- Catholics are expected to attend Mass each week.
- The Mass is the main form of worship for Catholics. It is one of the sacraments.
- The main part of the service is when the Eucharist, the bread and wine, are received by the congregation.
- Catholics believe the bread and wine become the body and blood of Jesus.

3.5 The Eucharist in other Christian traditions

Learning outcomes

At the end of this lesson you should be able to:

- describe the meaning of the act of commemoration
- explain why there are differences between Eucharist services
- explain why some Christians do not have a Eucharist service
- evaluate different points of view about the Eucharist.

edexcel ⠿ key terms

Commemoration – The belief that the Eucharist remembers and keeps alive the Last Supper of Jesus, but nothing happens to the bread and wine.

Sacred texts

'The Last Supper' (Luke 22:14–23)

What is being remembered by wearing a poppy? What other important events are remembered by people today?

Why are there different ways of celebrating the Eucharist?

Different Christians understand the Eucharist in different ways because of their different beliefs. Some Christians, for example the Quakers, do not celebrate the Eucharist. Among other Christians there are differences in the way it is celebrated and in the name it is given. The word 'Eucharist' means thanksgiving. The receiving of the bread and wine is an act of thanksgiving for the death and resurrection of Jesus.

For discussion

Do you think it is important to remember the Last Supper?

Activities

1 Read either Mark 14:16–26 or Luke 22:14–23. Imagine you were one of the disciples and write your diary entry describing the Last Supper.

What event is taking place here? Why is this an important event for Christians?

The Eucharist in the Baptist Church

The Baptist service is less formal, has no set order and can vary from church to church. It is called the Lord's Supper, and is usually held once or twice a month. The service starts with the minister calling the people to take the bread and wine in memory of the Last Supper and the death of Jesus. An account of the Last Supper is read over the bread and wine. It is an act of remembrance. Ordinary bread and grape juice are usually used. They are seen only as symbols of Jesus's presence. The people remain in their seats as the bread is handed out and the wine or grape juice is given to them in small cups, taken to them by the elders of the church. They all drink at the same time to show a sense of unity; all one in Jesus.

For discussion

How is this service different from the Catholic Mass?

Activities

2 Make up a table to show the similarities and differences between the Catholic Mass and the Lord's Supper.

Challenge

3 'Meaningful symbols can become meaningless rituals.' Do you agree?

The Salvation Army and the Eucharist

The Salvation Army does not use sacraments in its form of worship. They believe it is possible to receive God's blessing without sharing in the Eucharist. For the Salvation Army a sacrament is an outward sign of an inner experience, and it is the inner experience that is the most important thing.

The main reasons for not taking the Eucharist are:

- Salvation comes from a direct personal relationship with God and there is no need for such rituals.
- Some churches do not allow women to administer the sacraments; the Salvation Army believe women should take an equal role in its ministry.
- Many early converts to the Salvation Army were alcoholics so it was not a good idea to tempt them with the wine used in the Eucharist.

The Eucharist in the Church of England

There are different views of the Eucharist in the Church of England. Some members of the Church have similar beliefs to Catholics. Other members believe in two sacraments (baptism and the Eucharist). Some have similar beliefs about the sacraments to some Nonconformists like the Baptists.

Summary

- Christians view the Eucharist in different ways.
- Nonconformist Churches such as the Baptist and Methodist Churches, believe the Eucharist is an act of remembrance of Jesus's Last Supper and the bread and wine are just symbols of his body and blood.
- Some Christians, like the Salvation Army and Quakers, do not believe that sharing in the Eucharist is necessary to bring you closer to God.

3.6 The features of Catholic churches

72

Learning outcomes

By the end of this lesson you should be able to:

● describe the main features of a Catholic church

● give your opinion, with a reason, about the features of a Catholic church

● explain why Catholic churches have certain features

● evaluate the importance and meaning of the features of a Catholic church.

What is a church?

A church is place of worship for Christians and a focal point for the Christian community. The features to be found in the church show the importance of certain beliefs for the different Christian churches.

The exterior of a Catholic church

Catholic churches can look very different, depending on when they were built and the part of the world where they are found. Most traditional churches are built in the shape of a cross, but some modern church buildings are circular. Most churches have a bell tower or a spire – sometimes both.

The inside of a Catholic church

How does this building differ from a traditional parish church? Why do you think this is?

Activities

1 In small groups, prepare a presentation to explain the main features of a Catholic church. You may wish to focus on one you have visited.

● *Altar*: The table on which the priest prepares the Mass.

● *Tabernacle*: Where the reserve sacrament (bread and wine) is kept.

● *Lectern*: The Bible is read from here.

● *Pulpit*: The sermon is delivered from here.

● *Font*: Where babies are baptised – the font is usually found at the side of the altar or at the back of the church.

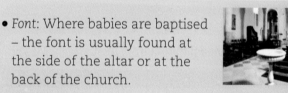

● *Confessional*: A small cubicle divided by a partition where the priest hears confessions.

● *The stoup*: A small container of blessed water that is placed near the entrance.

● *Stations of the Cross*: On the walls around the church are fourteen pictures that tell the story of Jesus's passion and death.

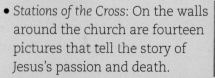

● *Statues*: Often there are a number of statues of Jesus, the Virgin Mary and the saints, such as St Peter.

For discussion

Which three features of a Catholic church do you think are the most important? Why?

What do these features mean?

All the features in a Catholic church are an expression of what is important to Catholics.

- The church in the shape of a cross is reminder of Jesus dying for the sins of the world. It faces east towards the rising sun as Jesus is seen as the light of the world.
- The altar is the focal point as this is where the priest consecrates the bread and wine. Catholic worship is 'altar centred 'and focuses on the sacrament of the Eucharist.
- The tabernacle represents the tent in which Moses kept the Ark of the Covenant that held the Ten Commandments. Jesus is believed to be the 'new covenant' ('covenant' means a contract or agreement), so the bread and wine that are left over from the Mass are placed in it.

Activities

2 Explain why you think some churches are now being built in a circular shape.

3 'It is waste of money making churches look beautiful.' Do you agree? Why?

4 Find out more about Catholic churches. Visit a local church or find a website that gives a virtual tour of a church building. You will find many books about church buildings in your local library. Most churches will have booklets with a guide to the features to be found there. Share you findings with your group.

Why do you think Catholics use statues in worship?

Activities

Challenge

5 'You shall not make for yourself an idol in the form of anything …' (Exodus 20:4) Do you think Catholics are breaking the second commandment? Give your reasons.

- The lectern and pulpit show that Catholics believe that the Bible and teachings of the Church are important but worship is centred on the celebration of the Eucharist.
- The font shows that Catholics believe that baptism is important; it is the first sacrament.
- Confessionals show that the sacrament of reconciliation is important as it is through the process of confession that Catholics can be reconciled with God.

Summary

- The focal points of a Catholic church are the altar and tabernacle. These show the importance of the sacrament of the Eucharist for Catholics.
- The presence of the font and confessionals highlight the significance of two of the other sacraments, baptism and reconciliation.

3.7 Why do Nonconformist Churches have certain features?

74

Lesson outcomes

By the end of this lesson you should be able to:

- describe the meaning of non-liturgical and charismatic worship
- give your opinion, with reasons, about the features of a Nonconformist Church
- explain why Nonconformist Churches have certain features
- evaluate the importance of certain features of the Nonconformist Church.

edexcel ⣿ key terms

Charismatic worship – Worship involving spiritual gifts such as speaking in tongues and healing.

Non-liturgical worship – Worship that does not have any set ritual or form of words.

Activities

1 Look at the picture of a Baptist church. Draw and label your own diagram using this photo as a reference.

2 From your study of the church, describe what you think Baptist worship is like.

3 Say what you think are the two most important features of the church.

Challenge

4 House church movement: some Christians look back to the times when the first Christians in the New Testament met in small groups in their own houses, so today they do the same. Why do you think house churches have developed?

The interior of a Baptist church. How does this building differ from a Catholic church? Why do you think this is?

ResultsPlus
Watch out!

- Some candidates forget to name the denomination of the church they are describing.
- Many candidates just describe the features rather than explain why the churches have these features.

Nonconformist Churches

Baptists, Methodists, the United Reform Church, Quakers, the Salvation Army and the Pentecostal Church are all Nonconformist Churches. Their worship tends to be **non-liturgical** and is planned according to the requirements of each congregation. For many Nonconformists, worship tends to be Bible-centred.

Quaker worship

Each Sunday morning at 10.30, members and visitors meet for an hour's silent worship at our Meeting House near Jesmond Metro station. An appointed Quaker will greet everyone as they enter. The Meeting itself starts as soon as the first person enters the Meeting Room. Benches and several chairs are arranged facing one another around the room. You may sit wherever you like. The Meeting gradually settles down into a deeper silence. At some point, one of those present may be moved to speak. On the central table are copies of various books including the *Bible* and a book of readings. Usually at Newcastle Meeting, which is typically attended by between forty and fifty people, several will speak or 'minister' during the course of the hour; but completely silent meetings are not unknown. At 11.30, or after a suitable interval following the last ministry, the elders shake hands to mark the end of the meeting. Notices are given out that include events planned for the following week, and occasionally reports from other meetings or conferences.

(Source: Extracts from Newcastle Quaker Meeting website, found at www.heinemann. co.uk/hotlinks (express code 4240P, link to 'Quakers in Newcastle').

Charismatic worship

Charismatic worship is spontaneous worship led by inspirations from the Holy Spirit. It is the main form of worship in the Pentecostal Church. A typical service would have hymns, gospel or pop-style music, prayers, Bible readings and a sermon. Quite often people dance and speak in tongues, as they feel moved by the Holy Spirit.

For discussion

Write down five words or phrases to describe this type of worship. What type of building would suit this type of worship?

Activities

5 **Role-play** In groups of four, each person takes on one of the following roles: a Catholic, a Baptist, a Quaker and a member of a Pentecostal church.

You have been asked to design a building that can be used by all Christians in the local community. You will need to present your design to the rest of the group.

For discussion

'You don't need a church to worship.' Do you agree?

Summary

- Nonconformist churches tend to be plain so that the worshippers are not distracted – this avoids breaking the commandment not to worship idols.

- For most Nonconformist Churches, worship tends to be Bible-centred, so the pulpit has a central place rather than the altar.

- The church provides a space for people to gather together to worship and is very plain and simple; communicating with God through quiet reflective prayer (Quakers) or lively spontaneous worship (Pentecostal Church) is what is important.

3.8 Christmas

Learning outcomes

By the end of this lesson you should be able to:

● describe the meaning of Advent and Christmas

● give your own opinion, with a reason, about Christmas

● explain why Christmas is important to Christians

● evaluate different points of view about Christmas.

edexcel ::: key terms

Advent – A time of spiritual preparation for Christmas.

What is Christmas?

The word 'Christmas' comes from Christ's Mass, the service held in the church to celebrate the birth of Jesus. For most Christians the festival begins on 25 December and lasts for twelve days.

Activities

1 Make a list of the Christmas customs that take place today. Decide which are religious and which are secular (non-religious).

2 Do you think Christmas has lost its true meaning today? Give two reasons for your answer.

3 In groups, read the gospel accounts of Jesus's birth.

4 Write the script for a nativity play. Perhaps you could perform it to another group or class.

5 Find out about the symbolism of the Advent wreath, sometimes called the Advent Crown.

6 Find out what happens at a Christingle service and the symbolism of the Christingle.

Why is Christmas a popular time?

How Christians celebrate Advent

Advent starts on the fourth Sunday before Christmas and ends on Christmas Eve. It is a time of spiritual preparation for Christmas. It is the time Christians start the countdown to Christmas. Advent calendars and candles help Christians to focus on the joyful anticipation of Christmas. Carol services are held during Advent and on the Sunday before Christmas. Many churches hold a service of Nine Lessons and Carols. Christingle services have become popular during Advent – these are especially popular with children. Nativity plays in schools and churches are often performed during the period up to Christmas.

Sacred texts

'The birth of Jesus and the visit of the Magi' (Matthew 1:18–2:12)

'The visit of the Shepherds' (Luke 2:1–20)

How Christians celebrate Christmas

Many churches and homes have cribs. A crib is a model of the stable where Jesus was born. The baby Jesus is placed in the manger on Christmas Eve. Crib services held in the afternoon of Christmas Eve have become popular. It is a service that involves and includes children.

- Many Christians will attend a Midnight Mass on Christmas Eve in candle-lit churches.
- On Christmas Day in the morning there is a family service at which the Gospel accounts of Jesus's birth will be read.
- Many Catholics will attend a Mass at dawn on Christmas Day to celebrate Jesus's coming into the world.
- Christians exchange gifts to remember the gifts given to Jesus by the Magi.
- Epiphany – the twelfth day and last day of Christmas – celebrates the visit of the Wise Men (the Three Kings) and their gifts to Jesus.

Why is Christmas important for Christians?

- It remembers the incarnation (see page 11), when God became man in the person of Jesus.
- It shows that God cared for the world so much that he sent his only Son to bring salvation for all (see page 14).
- It is through Jesus's death and resurrection that our sins can be forgiven and eternal life is made possible; without Jesus's birth this could not have happened.
- It is a special time for families, as Jesus was born into a human family.
- It is time to reflect on the meaning of peace and goodwill to all, as Jesus showed the world how people could live together in peace.

ResultsPlus
Top tip!

Remember always to refer to Christianity when answering (d)-type questions, otherwise you cannot get more than half marks.

1914 'football truce' anniversary

At Christmas 1914, during the First World War, the British soldiers played the German soldiers at football. The soldiers sang carols as they left the trenches to play football in sub-zero temperatures in 'no man's land', on the battlefields of France. For a short time no gunfire could be heard.

For discussion

- Why do you think the 'truce' took place at Christmas?
- 'It is important for Christians to believe Jesus's birth was special.' Do you agree?

Activities

7 Imagine you work for a Christian charity and are running a campaign at Christmas to raise funds for a major project. Write a radio jingle to encourage people to support your project.

Summary

- Christians celebrate Jesus's birth as it reminds them that God's Son became a man and lived on Earth.
- Christians believe that without Jesus there would be no Christianity and no salvation.
- Christians attend church services at Christmas that help them remember and celebrate the joy, love and peace Jesus brought to humankind.
- Christmas is an opportunity to show Christian love to others.

3.9 Lent

Learning outcomes

At the end of this lesson you should be able to:

- describe the meaning of Lent
- give your own opinion, with a reason, about Lent
- explain why Lent is important to Christians
- evaluate different points of view about Lent.

For discussion

Look at the cartoon. Why do you think people might give up certain things at Lent?

edexcel ::: key terms

Lent – The 40 days leading up to Easter.

What is Lent?

Lent is the period of forty days that lead up to Easter. Lent starts on Ash Wednesday and ends on Maundy Thursday. Lent is a time of reflection when Christians focus on God and spiritual matters in preparation for Easter. Jesus spent 40 days fasting in the desert before he started his ministry. Most Christians believe Jesus's time in the desert is the reason for the duration of Lent. Christians use Lent as a time for prayer and fasting.

Fasting during Lent

Most Christians try to give up something during Lent such as a favourite food or a bad habit. This is a test of self-discipline. Often the money saved from giving up things is donated to a charity. Some Christians use Lent as a time to think about others – the poor, homeless and needy. Many Christians increase their contributions to their favourite charities or get involved with directly helping others.

Activities

1 In pairs, think of five benefits of giving up something during Lent.

2 Read the story of Jesus in the desert. Write a text message summarising what happened.

Sacred texts

'The temptation of Jesus'
(Matthew 4:1–11; Luke 4:1–13)

Why is Ash Wednesday important for Christians?

On Ash Wednesday in the Catholic and Anglican Churches a service is held at which the congregation are marked on the forehead with a cross of ashes. The ashes are from the palms used for the Palm Sunday celebrations (see page 80). The ash cross is a symbol of penitence. As the priest marks the cross on the forehead he says:

> **Sacred texts**
>
> 'Almighty God, you have created us out of the dust of the Earth: Grant that these ashes may be to us a sign of our mortality and penitence ... Remember that you are dust, and to dust you shall return.'

The marking of the forehead with the cross reminds Christians that:

- they should regret their sins and try to change for the better
- God created humans by breathing life into dust; without God humans are nothing but dust and ashes
- Jesus was sacrificed on the cross as atonement for all the sins of the world
- Ash Wednesday helps Christians to focus on the 'Lenten' practices – prayer, fasting and concern for others.

Why is Lent important for Christians?

- During Lent Christians reflect upon their baptismal vows (see page 62). The cross of ashes acts as a reminder of the cross made upon their foreheads at baptism.
- Lent is a time when Christians think about how they can improve their Christian life. They try to spend more time in prayer. Often there are special Lenten study groups to help them think about their faith.
- It is a time when the Christian community comes together and grows in faith through prayer, study and services.
- It is a time to think about others and get involved in charity work. This helps each Christian to feel part of a wider Christian community.

Activities

3 Draw an ash cross and inside it include the beliefs and ideas that Christians should be reminded of during Lent. You can use words or pictures or both.

4 Explain why Lent is an important time of year for Christians

5 Explain why a Christian might support the work of a charity such as CAFOD, Christian Aid or Tear Fund, especially during Lent.

To find out about the work of charitable organisations, go to www.heinemann. co.uk/hotlinks (express code 4240P), and use the links to 'CAFOD', Christian Aid or Tear Fund. You could also read some of the many booklets and other information that these organisations produce.

Challenge

6 What is Mardi Gras? How is this linked with Lent?

For discussion

'Giving to charity is the most important part of Lent.' Do you agree?

Summary

- Lent is the 40 days before Easter, starting on Ash Wednesday when a special service is held.
- During Lent, Christians remember the time Jesus spent in the desert before he started his ministry.
- During Lent Christians give up things, spend more time in prayer, and meet with others to reflect on their faith in preparation for the celebration of Easter.

3.10 Holy Week – Palm Sunday and Maundy Thursday

Learning outcomes

At the end of this lesson you should be able to:

- describe the meaning of Palm Sunday and Maundy Thursday
- give your own opinion, with a reason, about Palm Sunday and Maundy Thursday
- explain why Palm Sunday and Maundy Thursday are important to Christians
- evaluate different points of view about Palm Sunday and Maundy Thursday.

edexcel ⠿ key terms

Holy Week – The week before Easter Sunday.

Sacred texts

'Jesus enters Jerusalem' (Mark 11:9–11)

What is Holy Week?

Holy Week is the week before Easter. It includes Palm Sunday, Maundy Thursday and Good Friday and ends on Holy Saturday, the day before Easter, at midnight. During this week Christians remember the events of the last week of Jesus's life.

What does Palm Sunday celebrate?

On Palm Sunday Christians remember when Jesus rode into Jerusalem on a donkey. The crowds gave him a triumphal welcome, waving palm branches and shouting his praises.

What does Maundy Thursday celebrate?

On this day Jesus and his disciples celebrated the Last Supper (see page 70). At this meal Jesus washed the feet of the disciples as a sign of his service to them. After the meal Jesus and the disciples went to the Garden of Gethsemane. As Jesus was praying, Judas Iscariot arrived with the soldiers to arrest him. During the night Jesus was put on trial before he was crucified the next day.

For discussion

Look at the photograph below. How do we know that these Christians are celebrating Palm Sunday?

Activities

1 In pairs, one of you is a reporter and the other a person who has just witnessed Jesus's entry into Jerusalem. The reporter now has to interview the witness as to what they have just seen and their views about it.

For discussion

Why do you think Jesus washed the feet of the disciples? What can Christians learn from this today?

How is Palm Sunday celebrated?

Some churches have a procession. The congregation carry large palm leaves and sometimes they have a donkey at the front of the procession. The congregation are often given small crosses made of dried palm leaves.

During the service the story of Jesus's Passion is read. Special hymns for Palm Sunday are sung.

How is Maundy Thursday celebrated?

- In some churches, during the service, the priest will wash the feet of twelve members of the congregation, to remember what Jesus did for the disciples at the Last Supper.
- In some churches, the altar cloth and ornaments are removed, symbolising how Jesus was deserted by the disciples in Gethsemane.
- In the Catholic Church, the blessed sacrament of bread and wine are removed from the tabernacle and stored on a side altar. Sometimes a watch (or vigil) is kept over the consecrated bread and wine up to Easter Day. The people are following Jesus's request to stay and pray with him as he asked the disciples to do. The bishop will consecrate the chrism, the oil, used in baptism.

Why are Palm Sunday and Maundy Thursday important?

Christians on Palm Sunday are remembering that Jesus is worthy of praise and that they believe him to be the Messiah (the promised Saviour). When Jesus rode into Jerusalem on a donkey he was saying by his actions that he was the long-awaited Messiah and was fulfilling the promise of the Old Testament.

Maundy Thursday is important as it reminds Christians of how the Eucharist started and the 'new covenant' between God and humans was established. The name 'Maundy' comes from the Latin meaning commandment. Being part of the old covenant meant following the Ten Commandments; Jesus gave the disciples a new commandment to 'love one another.' The washing of the feet acts as a reminder to everyone to love and serve others.

Sacred texts

'The authority of Jesus' (Matthew 21:5)

'Jesus washes the disciples' feet' (John 13:34–5)

For discussion

What is the Queen doing in the photograph? Why is she doing this?

Summary

- Holy Week is the week before Easter and includes Palm Sunday, Maundy Thursday and Good Friday.
- On Palm Sunday Christians are given palm crosses to remember the day Jesus rode into Jerusalem on a donkey, but was greeted as a king.
- On Maundy Thursday Christians remember the Last Supper and how Jesus washed the disciples' feet as a sign of his service to them.

Activities

2 Create a diagram to show the symbolism used on Palm Sunday and Maundy Thursday. You can use words and pictures.

Challenge

3 The feet washing ceremony is no longer relevant today. Do you agree?

3.11 Holy Week – Good Friday

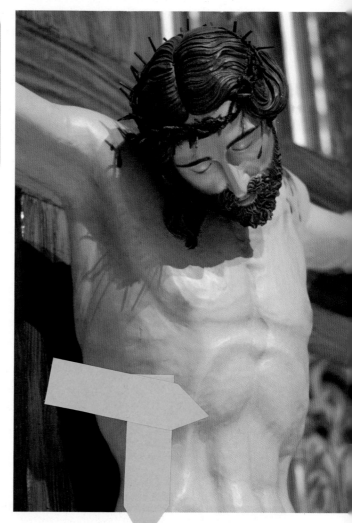

What is 'good' about Good Friday?

Learning outcomes

At the end of this lesson you should be able to:

- describe the meaning of Good Friday
- give your opinion, with reasons, about Good Friday
- explain why Good Friday is important to Christians
- evaluate the importance of Good Friday for Christians.

What is Good Friday?

Good Friday is the most important day of Holy Week. It is the day when Christians remember the crucifixion of Jesus. It is a day of mourning when they meditate on Jesus's suffering and death and what it means to them.

What does Good Friday remember?

On this day Jesus was taken before Pontius Pilate and was sentenced to death. He was beaten and mocked before being made to carry his own cross to the place of crucifixion. He was nailed to the cross. He hung there for many hours until he died. Jesus was then removed from the cross and placed in a tomb on the same day.

What do Christians do on Good Friday?

- In some churches the pictures and statues are removed or are covered with a black cloth and there are no flowers.
- Some Christians hold 'Processions of Witness' – a procession following behind someone carrying a large wooden cross, to represent Jesus.
- There is a special service to remember the crucifixion. The four Gospel accounts of the crucifixion are read.
- A large wooden cross is brought into the church for all to see, special prayers are said and the congregation are invited to kiss the cross as an act of reverence.

Sacred texts

'The death of Jesus' (Matthew 15:1–41; Mark 15:21–41; Luke 23:26–49; John 19:17–42)

For discussion

The Procession of Witness often goes round local streets and members of different churches all walk together. What do you think this shows?

Activities

1 Make a list of ten words that describe what the church would look and feel like on Good Friday.

2 Explain why Good Friday is described as a day of mourning.

The Eucharist on Good Friday

In many churches there is no Eucharist on Good Friday. In others, the bread and wine are not consecrated but taken from that put aside on Maundy Thursday (see pages 80–81). This is a way of showing that Jesus had been taken away from his people.

The Stations of the Cross

In a Catholic church the fourteen Stations of the Cross are found around the walls. These stations were placed in churches when it became dangerous for pilgrims to visit Via Dolorosa in Jerusalem. This was the route that Jesus took from the city to his place of crucifixion. On Good Friday Catholics stand in front of each of the stations and listen to what happened at each stage of Jesus's journey to the cross. They offer prayers and reflect on what Jesus suffered for the sake of humankind.

Activities

Challenge

3 Dali set the picture of the crucifixion in his own village and his wife is standing at the foot of the cross. Why do you think Dali set the picture here and included his wife? What message about Good Friday do you think the picture gives to Christians today?

Why is Good Friday important?

This day acts as a reminder of the pain, suffering and sacrifice of Jesus. It gives each Christian an inner strength to face the suffering they may have to cope with in their own lives.

The death of Jesus made it possible for all to achieve salvation; the sins of the world could be forgiven.

Activities

4 In a group, find out what each of the fourteen Stations of the Cross represent. Which three do you think are the most significant?

5 Find out what happens on Holy Saturday in the Catholic Church. How does this help Christians prepare for Easter?

6 'Good Friday is more important than Christmas.'
Do you agree?

ResultsPlus
Top tip!

Remember that Good Friday is in Holy Week and is not part of Easter, so remember not to write about it if the question asks about how or why Easter is celebrated.

Summary

- Good Friday remembers the crucifixion and suffering of Jesus.
- Christians hold Processions of Witness and special services in the church during which the Gospel accounts of Jesus's death are read.
- Good Friday is important as it reminds Christians that through Jesus's death and sacrifice salvation from sin is possible.

3.12 Easter

> ## Learning outcomes
>
> At the end of this lesson you should be able to:
>
> - describe the meaning of Easter
> - give your own opinion, with reasons, about Easter
> - explain why Easter is important to Christians
> - evaluate the importance of Easter for Christians.

What is Easter?

Easter is the festival that celebrates the resurrection of Jesus. It takes place on the Sunday following Good Friday. It is the most important festival for Christians. This is the day Jesus conquered death and came back to life, giving Christians hope and faith that death is not the end of everything.

What does Easter remember?

On the third day after Jesus's death, some of the women who followed him went to visit his tomb. They found the tomb was empty. A figure dressed in white clothes told them that Jesus had risen from the dead, and to go and tell the disciples. The disciples did not believe the women until they saw the risen Jesus for themselves.

What do Christians do at Easter?

In many churches an Easter vigil is held. It starts some time on Holy Saturday after it has got dark. Late into the evening, outside the church, a fire is lit and the Paschal Candle is lit from it and carried into the darkened church. Often the congregation will have their own candles that they will light from the Paschal Candle as it is carried past.

The church is decorated with flowers and the priest will wear white or gold. In many churches an Easter garden will be built. This is a model of Jesus's tomb as described in the Gospels.

On Easter Day (Easter Sunday) passages from the Bible on the Easter theme are read. Joyful hymns are sung and the Eucharist is received by the congregation.

For discussion

- What Easter symbols can you see in this card? Would a Christian say this was a suitable card for Easter?
- Do you think chocolate Easter eggs are a true Christian symbol of Easter?

Sacred texts

'The resurrection of Jesus' (Luke 24:1–12)

Activities

1 Write a text message sent by one of the women after visiting the tomb and the reply from one of the disciples.

2 Draw a design for your own Easter garden with some accompanying notes to describe the features of your garden.

The symbolism of the Paschal Candle

Jesus is the light of the world and was sent by God to rescue humankind from their sins

The five pieces of incense or brass symbolise the wounds on Jesus's body

The numbers are the four numbers of the year. This symbolises that Jesus is present now and always will be

The candle is a symbol of new life and is used throughout the year at baptisms

Alpha and Omega (the first and last letters of the Greek alphabet) show that Jesus is the beginning and end of all things

Why is Easter important to Christians?

- The belief in the resurrection of Jesus is central to the Christian message. The resurrection of Jesus proved that Jesus was the Son of God, as only God had the power rise from the dead.
- It gives Christians the hope that death is not the end and that there is life after death. As Jesus rose from the dead, so will those who believe in him.
- The resurrection shows that Jesus is still alive and working through the Church. Christians today believe they can still meet Jesus through prayer and worship.
- It is a time that Christians reflect on the meaning of their faith. Some Christians will renew their baptismal vows at this time of year.

Activities

Challenge

3 Easter Monday has become a day when campaign groups such as CND choose to hold protest marches. Why do you think they chose this day? Is it the right way for Christians to observe Easter?

Activities

4 Find out about how Easter is celebrated in the Orthodox Church. How is this similar to other Churches? How is it different? Why?

5 Imagine you are a priest and you have been asked to write an article for the parish magazine on the meaning of Easter today for Christians. Write your article.

For discussion

'Christianity is the religion of Easter.' Do you agree? Why?

Summary

- Easter is when Christians celebrate the resurrection of Jesus.
- Worship is joyful. Many symbols such as the Paschal Candle and eggs are used to show the meaning of new life at Easter.
- The resurrection of Jesus is the evidence for Christians that Jesus was the Son of God and gives them the hope of eternal life.

Know Zone
Section 3:
Worship and celebration

Quick quiz

1 Name two symbols used in the infant baptism service.

2 Give two reasons why confirmation is important for Christians.

3 What does transubstantiation mean?

4 What event does the Eucharist remember?

5 Name four features found inside a Catholic church.

6 What is charismatic worship?

7 Give two reasons why Christmas is important for Christians.

8 When does Lent start and end?

9 What does Good Friday remember?

10 Give two reasons why Easter is important for Christians.

Plenary activities

1 Design a mind map to summarise the Christian festivals you have studied.

2 Write your quick quiz questions on the Christian places of worship you have studied. Give them to another member of your class to do and you can mark it for them.

3 Make up a table to show the similarities and differences between believers' baptism and confirmation.

Student tip

- Remember that some people call infant baptism a christening.

- Don't use the phrase 'all Christians' when referring to the Mass or Eucharist, as different Christian groups hold different beliefs about it. If you cannot name the group of Christians, use the words 'some' or 'others'.

- You need to know why the churches you have studied have certain features. You need to say how the features reflect the beliefs and what is important to each group of Christians.

- Remember that Holy Week refers to Palm Sunday, Maundy Thursday and Good Friday, not Easter.

- When answering a question about Christmas, you must refer to the importance of Christmas for Christians not just why many others choose to celebrate it today.

Self-evaluation checklist

Read through the following list and evaluate how well you know and understand each of the topics.
How well have you understood the topics in this section? In the first column of the table below use the following code to rate your understanding:

Green – I understand this fully

Orange – I am confident I can answer most questions on this

Red – I need to do a lot more work on this topic.

In the second and third columns you need to think about:

- Whether you have an opinion on this topic and could give reasons for that opinion if asked
- Whether you can give the opinion of someone who disagrees with you and give reasons for this alternative opinion.

Content covered	My understanding is red/orange/ green	Can I give my opinion?	Can I give an alternative opinion?
The meaning and importance for Christians of infant and adult baptism and confirmation			
The meaning and importance for Christians of the Mass or Eucharist.			
The meaning and importance for Christians of Christmas, Lent, Holy Week and Easter.			
Why Roman Catholic churches and Nonconformist churches have certain features.			

Find out more

- The BBC website contains a lot of useful information about baptism, confirmation, the Eucharist and the festivals. Go to www.heinemann.co.uk/hotlinks (express code 4240P) and click on the link for Religions.
- If you are unable to visit different churches, church websites often have pictures of their church and some will give a virtual tour.
- Depending on the time of year, there are television programmes that show how Christians celebrate the Christian festivals in church.
- The Church of England website gives lots of information to people considering baptism or confirmation. Go to www.heinemann.co.uk/hotlinks (express code 4240P) and click on the link for the Church of England.
- You could arrange a visit to see how the Eucharist is celebrated in different churches.
- Websites such as REfuel and RE:Quest have a lot of resources about the Christian festivals.

Know Zone
Section 3: Worship and celebration

In the exam you need to answer four questions, one from each section. The examination is one hour and 30 minutes. Spend a few minutes reading through the whole examination paper carefully, and decide which questions you are going to answer. You should allow about 20 minutes to answer each question.

The bold type tells you this is one of the key term glossary terms.

In these questions, make sure you write about the topic set. If you write a perfect answer about adult baptism you would get no marks.

Mini Exam Paper

(a) What is **Holy Week**? (2 marks)

(b) Do you think people should give things up for Lent?

Give **two** reasons for your point of view. (4 marks)

(c) Explain why many Christians practise infant baptism. (8 marks)

(d) 'Christmas is the most important festival.'

In your answer you should refer to Christianity.

(i) Do you agree? Give reasons for your opinion. (3 marks)

(ii) Give reason why some people might disagree with you. (3 marks)

The reasons you give do not have to be from a religious viewpoint.

You can get full marks by giving three simple reasons to each part of the question.

Results Plus
Watch out!

In answers to questions about the festivals make sure you refer to how and why Christians celebrate the festivals and not how non-religious people keep these festivals today.

In your answers make it clear which Christian tradition you are writing about, especially when answering questions about the Eucharist and the features of different Churches.

Support activity

1 Try answering this examination question in 20 mins.

(a) What is advent? (2 marks)

(b) Should Christians be baptised as babies?

Give two reasons for your point of view. (4 marks)

(c) Explain why a Catholic church has certain features. (8 marks)

(d) 'All Christians should celebrate the Eucharist in the same way.'

(i) Do you agree? Give reasons for your opinion. (3 marks)

(ii) Give reasons why some people might disagree with you. (3 marks)

Results Plus

Maximise your marks

(c) Explain why many Christians practise infant baptism. (8 marks)

Student answer	Examiner comments	Build a better answer
Many christens have there babies baptised coz they want there child to be bought up as a christen and to give them a christen name. It takes place around the font and the vicer pours water on the baby head and it wares white.	This candidate has given one reason – because the parents want the child brought up as a Christian. The rest of the answer is just description, so gains no marks. In (c)-type questions, marks are awarded for the quality of your written communication. As there are a number of spelling errors in this answer, the candidate will be awarded the lower mark in the level. This is a Level 1 answer so it can get 1 or 2 marks. Because of the poor spelling it will be given 1 mark.	Many Christians have their babies baptised because they want them to be brought up as a Christian. The service takes place around the font and water from the font is poured on the baby's head. This is important because it represents the washing away of sin, so the baby is starting a new life with God. As Jesus was baptised the parents want to follow his example for their baby. Many Christians believe that through baptism the Holy Spirit enters the life of the child so they want this to happen as soon as possible.

Living the Christian life

Introduction

In this section you will explore, think and learn about living the Christian life. This will include looking at the idea of Christian vocation, how the Ten Commandments and the Sermon on the Mount act as a guide for living, and how and why one Christian organisation works for the relief of poverty and suffering in the UK.

Learning outcomes for this section

By the end of this section, you should be able to:

● give definitions of the key terms and use them in answer to GCSE questions

● describe how Christians can show vocation in their lives

● state the teachings of the Ten Commandments and the Law of Moses, and how displaying religion, money, judgement and the Golden Rule were re-interpreted in the Sermon on the Mount

● describe how Christians work for social and community cohesion and look at how one Christian organisation helps to relieve poverty and/or suffering

● explain why Christians show vocation, either in their daily life or by taking holy orders

● explain why Christians use the Ten Commandments as a guide for living

● explain why Christians use the teachings on re-interpretation of the Law of Moses, displaying religion, money, judgement and the Golden Rule from the Sermon on the Mount as a guide for living

● explain why Christians work for social and community cohesion and how one Christian organisation helps to relieve poverty and suffering

● express your own point of view about Christian vocation, the teachings found in the Ten Commandments and the Sermon on the Mount, and the work of a Christian organisation, giving your reasons

● evaluate points of view about living the Christian life today, showing that you have thought about different views from your own, giving reasons and evidence

● describe the meaning of vocation and its importance for Christians

● explain how and why Christians show vocation in their daily lives and some Christians take holy orders

● explain how and why some Christians are involved in working for social and community cohesion

● describe how and why Christians use the Ten Commandments as a guide for living

● explain how and why Christians use the re-interpretation of the Law of Moses in the Sermon on the Mount on displaying religion, money, judgement and the Golden Rule as a guide for living

● describe how and why one Christian organisation helps to relieve poverty and suffering in the UK.

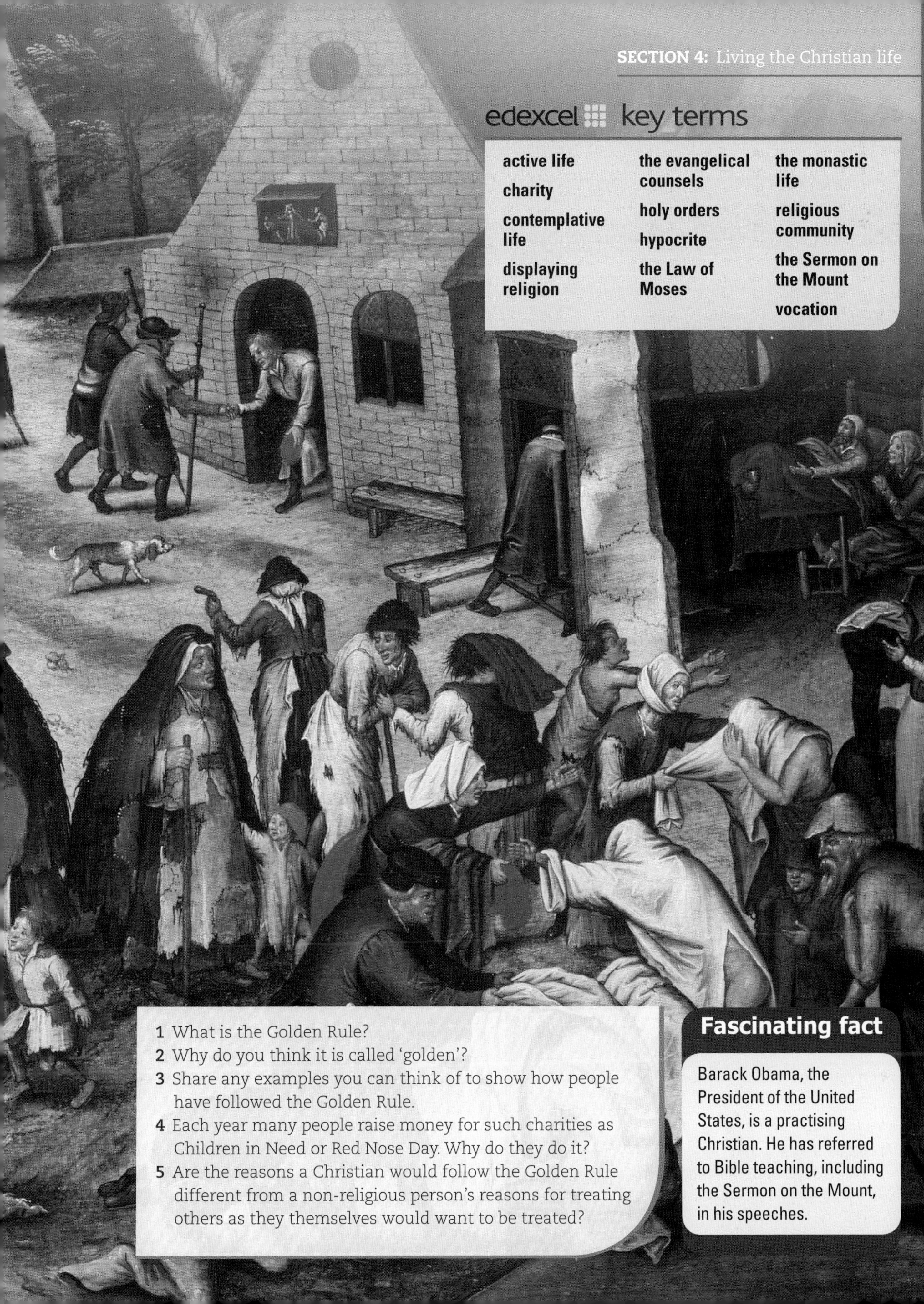

edexcel ⠿ key terms

active life	the evangelical counsels	the monastic life
charity	holy orders	religious community
contemplative life	hypocrite	the Sermon on the Mount
displaying religion	the Law of Moses	vocation

91

1 What is the Golden Rule?
2 Why do you think it is called 'golden'?
3 Share any examples you can think of to show how people have followed the Golden Rule.
4 Each year many people raise money for such charities as Children in Need or Red Nose Day. Why do they do it?
5 Are the reasons a Christian would follow the Golden Rule different from a non-religious person's reasons for treating others as they themselves would want to be treated?

Fascinating fact

Barack Obama, the President of the United States, is a practising Christian. He has referred to Bible teaching, including the Sermon on the Mount, in his speeches.

4.1 What is vocation?

Learning outcomes

By the end of this lesson you should be able to:

● describe the meaning of vocation, the monastic life and the evangelical counsels

● give your own opinion, with a reason, about the active and the contemplative life

● explain why vocation is important for Christians

● evaluate the importance of different types of vocation for Christians.

For discussion

How is the person in the picture below following Jesus's teachings? How do you think they are showing they have a vocation?

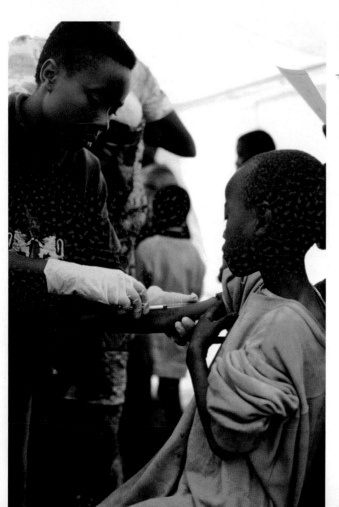

edexcel ⬚ key terms

Active life – The life lived by religious orders who work in society as well as praying.

Contemplative life – The life of prayer and meditation lived by some religious orders.

The evangelical counsels – The vows of poverty, chastity and obedience.

The monastic life – Living as a monk or nun in a religious community.

Religious community – A religious order who live together as a group, e.g. the Benedictines.

Vocation – A call from God to lead the Christian life.

Activities

1 Complete the following sentence with five bullet points: 'Being a disciple of Jesus means…'

2 Explain how one religious community shows service to God.

Sacred texts

'*Giving the disciples power*' (Matthew 10:1)

What does vocation mean?

The word **vocation** comes from the Latin word to 'call'. Christians believe they are called to be followers of Jesus and to live their life in a Christian way. Christians show their vocation in a variety of ways:

● by living the Christian life and showing their love of God and others

● by becoming a priest

● by becoming a member of a religious community, and being a monk or a nun

● through their work – for example, joining the caring professions

● through marriage and raising a family

● by being a disciple today.

Christians often refer to their vocation as 'discipleship'. A disciple is a follower of Jesus. All Christians are asked to follow the teachings of Jesus, just as the first disciples did. In their daily lives they must be a witness to the love of God and others in the way they worship God and treat other people.

For discussion

Do you think non-religious people can have a vocation?

Active life versus contemplative life

The **contemplative life** is one where people separate themselves from society and spend their time in prayer. As they are not distracted by the demands of the world, they can devote themselves to building a relationship with God. They believe this is the way they can help the world today.

The **active life** means that people choose to live in a **religious community** but do not separate themselves from the rest of the world. Prayer is a very important part of their daily life, but they believe they should serve others too. By serving others they are a witness to God for all the world to see, and are working to make the world a better place as they believe God would have wanted.

Why choose the monastic life?

'My parish was served by Franciscans, and as a teenager I was inspired by the dedicated life of one of the young Franciscans and wanted to be like him. So I became a Franciscan. But some years on, I went on retreat to a Benedictine monastery, and found myself more attracted to the discipline of the monastic life, the balance between work and prayer, the way I was uplifted by the singing of plainchant. So I became a monk! I think my parents felt I just didn't know what I wanted, but then I think life is more about searching than finding.'
Dom Stephen

The monastic life

Some Christians choose to show their vocation through choosing the **monastic life** and devoting their life completely to God. When they become a member of the religious community they take three vows known as the **evangelical counsels**.

- *Vow of poverty*: They give up all their possessions and any money earned goes to the community.
- *Vow of chastity*: They dedicate themselves to God so do not marry or have any sexual relationship.
- *Vow of obedience*: They must do as the person in charge of the community tells them, and when making any decisions they must refer to the members of the community.

To find out more about the life led by different religious communities, go to www.heinemann.co.uk/hotlinks (express code 4240P, link to 'Carmelite Nuns', 'Benedictine Monks', or 'Salesians').

For discussion

'The vows of poverty, chastity and obedience are no longer relevant.' Do you agree?

Summary

- Christian vocation is a call to discipleship.
- Vocation can be seen through marriage, family life and work.
- Some Christians choose to show their vocation by joining a religious community or becoming a priest.

4.2 Vocation in daily life and work

Learning outcomes

By the end of this lesson you should be able to:

- give examples of how Christians show vocation in their daily life and work
- give your own opinion, with a reason, about how Christians show vocation in their daily life and work
- explain how and why Christians show vocation in their daily life and work
- evaluate the importance of vocation in the daily life and work of Christians.

Marriage and family life as a vocation

For Christians, family life is very important and it helps to hold society together. Therefore, to marry and have children is seen as a vocation equally as important as joining a religious community. By having a Christian wedding, the couple are making a public declaration of their commitment to each other in the presence of God. They are showing that they believe in God and are committed to showing Christian values in their life together.

By bringing up children in a Christian family the parents are acting as disciples and teaching the faith to their children.

Showing vocation in daily life

Christians can show their vocation in their everyday lives by following Christian values. This can be shown in small acts, like helping out an elderly neighbour, supporting friends in need, or spending time raising funds for a charitable cause.

Showing vocation through work

Many Christians choose jobs that enable them to show the important Christian values of service and compassion to others, for example as a doctor, teacher or social worker. Others may choose a career that involves sharing the message of Jesus with others, such as a charity or missionary worker.

For discussion

The film *Billy Elliot* tells the story of an 11-year-old coal miner's son in the North of England. His life changes when, by chance, he goes to a ballet class. Before long he finds himself immersed in ballet and finds out that he is very talented. He has a dream to go to ballet school. Billy achieves this and leaves home to start his life as a dancer. How can his story help someone to understand what vocation is?

Activities

1 In pairs, make a list of the varieties of ways a Christian can show their vocation.

For discussion

Do you think you need to be single to show a true vocation?

Vocation at work

Christians not only show their vocation by their choice of career but by showing Christian values in the work they do. In their jobs, Christians believe they should be honest and treat others fairly. If they are an employer, they should not exploit or treat their employees in an unfair way. As an employee, they should give a fair day's work in return for a fair wage.

Some Christians show their vocation by actively not working for companies that make a profit at the expense of others or the environment, for example, by not working for a company that exploits cheap labour in the developing world or that directly harms the environment.

Call to discipleship

Some Christians decide it is their vocation to help and serve others who are in real need in this country or abroad. They often give up their job and lifestyle and work in the areas of most need in the world. They often work for such organisations as Christian Aid or CAFOD. They believe they are following Jesus's call to discipleship.

For discussion

Are there any jobs a Christian should not do?

Marriage as a call to witness

Christians describe their vocation as a 'call to witness'. This means that they show their faith in God and Jesus and the power of the Holy Spirit in the way they live their lives. Marriage is seen as a witness to faith as the couple make their vows in the presence of God. For Catholic Christians it is one of the sacraments, so it is an act of witness to their faith in God.

Family life itself acts as a witness to the faith because they are showing love for each other in the way God requires them to do.

For discussion

'The best vocation for a Christian is to become a member of a religious community.' Do you agree?

Activities

3 Write a text message or email to explain to someone what vocation means to a Christian.

4 Explain how Christians show the call to discipleship in their daily lives.

Activities

Challenge

2 Many churches hold a Vocations Sunday service. Find out more about this. How does it show the importance of vocation for Christians?

To find out more about Vocations Sunday, go to www.heinemann.co.uk/hotlinks (express code 4240P, link to 'Vocations').

Summary

- For many Christians, marriage and family life are a way of showing vocation, the call to discipleship and witness.
- Christians can also show vocation by their choice of career or work and how they treat others in their daily lives.

4.3 Taking holy orders

96

NO ONE IS BORN A PRIEST

It takes a community to raise a priest; from families who talk about vocations, to parishioners who pray for and champion religious life, to priests themselves, who through their lives of compassion and sacrifice, reveal Christ's abundant love. if you know someone who would make a good priest, tell him. And ask him to call our Vocational Office. Your encouragement could make all the difference.

(904) 262-3200, ext. 101 • www.dosafl.com • email: vocations@dosafl.com

THE DIOCESE OF SAINT AUGUSTINE

For discussion

What do you think 'no one is born a priest' means?

Taking holy orders

Some Christians feel they are called to become a priest or minister within their Church. They show their vocation by taking **holy orders**.

Becoming a priest involves a long period of training before they are 'ordained' into the ministry. Once they are ordained as a priest, it is their role to celebrate the sacraments, teach and preach, and ensure all members of their church are cared for (see pages 50–51).

A way of showing discipleship

Becoming a priest is a way of showing you are a true disciple of Jesus. Being a priest requires:

- a love of God
- love of the Eucharist (see pages 70–71) and prayer
- a commitment to living the Christian life by obeying the commandments
- wanting to share the teachings of Jesus with others
- a belief in the importance of the Church and its teachings
- the willingness to dedicate your life to the service of God and others.

For discussion

- Do you think women in the Catholic Church should be able to show their vocation by becoming priests?
- 'The greatest calling for a Christian is to be a priest.' Do you agree?

Activities

1 Make your own list of reasons why you think someone might want to become a priest.

2 Either interview someone who has become a priest or find a story on the Internet about someone who has chosen this calling. Explain how these individuals have shown vocation, and what led them to answer the calling to be a priest.

What other roles can a priest take on besides being a parish priest?

Being called to be a priest

Some Christians feel they are called to be a priest. They believe this is what God wants them to do with their life. In the New Testament the disciples were called to follow Jesus. Being called can be described as an inner feeling that one knows what God wants you to do.

During the ordination service in the Catholic Church, priests are asked if they wish to serve God's people. They reply 'I am ready and willing.' The call is to serve and not be served; it is about putting God first.

Sacred texts

'Jesus tells the disciples to go and spread his teaching' (Matthew 28:19)

'Jesus heals a paralysed man' (Luke 5:17–26)

'The Last Supper' (Luke 42:14–23)

Activities

Challenge

3   During the ordination service the bishop says: 'Priests are called to be servants and shepherds among the people to whom they are sent.' Why do you think priests are described as servants and shepherds?

To find more information about the priesthood go to www.heinemann.co.uk/hotlinks (express code 4240P, link to 'UK priest' or 'Church of England').

Continuing Jesus's ministry

- Jesus commanded the disciples to go and make disciples of all nations and baptise them. Today, it is the priest who performs the sacrament of baptism.
- Jesus forgave people's sins. It is the priest who hears confessions and grants forgiveness.
- There are many occasions when Jesus visited people. He took his message to them. The priest today works in the community, visiting the sick, the elderly, hospitals, schools and those in prison.
- At the Last Supper Jesus instructed his disciples to take the bread and wine 'in remembrance of me.' Only those who have taken holy orders can prepare the sacrament of the Eucharist so that Jesus's command can be carried out.

Why take holy orders?

It just made sense to me at the time. I couldn't see myself doing anything else with my life.

Some people feel the need to help and serve others through being something like a doctor. I felt I needed to serve God and others through becoming a priest.

I was struggling to find a direction in my life and I prayed. Gradually the answer came to me that my vocation was to take holy orders.

It is my way of showing my love of God, Jesus and the Church.

Summary

- Some Christians believe it is their vocation to take holy orders and become a priest.
- Through being a priest they are continuing the ministry of Jesus in the world today.

4.4 Working for social and community cohesion

Learning outcomes

By the end of this lesson you should be able to:

- describe the meaning of social and community cohesion
- give your own opinion, with reasons, about Christians working for social and community cohesion
- explain how and why Christians work for social and community cohesion
- evaluate the importance of Christians working for social and community cohesion.

For discussion

During the summer of 2001 there were a series of racially motivated riots in a number of towns in the UK, including Bradford. Why do you think this made people believe they needed to work harder for community cohesion?

Working for community cohesion in the local community

Many Christians believe it is important to work to make their local community a better place for everyone to live in. The needs of the local community will vary for different areas, but Christians believe they should work towards:

- equality of opportunities for all
- valuing different people's backgrounds
- fostering a sense of belonging.

This means challenging any form of prejudice and discrimination and looking for ways of bringing people together to foster good relationships.

Activities

1   Write a one-minute speech explaining why Christians should work for community cohesion in their local community. Deliver your speech to the rest of the class.

For discussion

'Community cohesion is the responsibility of the government, not Christians.' Do you agree?

Why Christians work for community cohesion

In the Bible there are many incidents and teachings showing how Jesus tried to bring about harmonious relationships between different groups. For example:

- the parable of the Good Samaritan (see pages 18–19) teaches Christians that they should treat all people, no matter what their background or race, as their neighbour
- Jesus healed a Roman centurion's servant and mixed with a Samaritan woman, showing that all people should be treated equally
- St Paul (in the New Testament book of Galatians) taught that all people are equal in Christ, so there should be no divisions in society.

Sacred texts

'The parable of the Good Samaritan' (Luke 10:25–37)

'Jesus heals a centurion's servant' (Luke 7:1–10)

'Jesus meets a Samaritan woman' (John 4)

'All are one in Christ' (Galatians 3:26–29)

Why do you think it is important for people from different faiths to come together?

Working for community cohesion in the UK

Inter-faith dialogue

Organisations have been set up for people from different religions to come together and share and celebrate their different faiths. The Inter-faith Network for the UK was founded in 1987 to promote good relations between the faith communities. There are many local branches of the group.

Working for economic justice

The group Church Action on Poverty works to tackle the causes of poverty. They also campaign for the wellbeing of refugees and asylum seekers in the UK today.

The Church working for racial equality

The Church of England's Committee for Minority and Ethnic Anglican Concerns (CMEC) works to encourage the participation of black Christian groups in the Church.

Sacred texts

'Humans created in the image of God' (Genesis 1:26)

'The meaning of Peter's vision' (Acts 10:34–35)

The world today

Christians believe it is important to help and support communities throughout the world where there are conflicts and inequalities. Many Christians support the work of such organisations as CAFOD (Catholic Association for Overseas Development) and Christian Aid, and some even choose to work for them. Besides providing emergency aid, they help local communities by building a better quality of life for all.

Christians believe they are part of the worldwide community because God was the Creator of all human beings and all are created in the image of God. In St Peter's vision (found in the New Testament book of Acts) he believed that God was showing him that God himself treats everyone equally, therefore Christians have a responsibility to do the same.

For more information about organisations such as Inter-Faith Network, Church Action on Poverty, CAFOD and Christian Aid promoting social and community cohesion worldwide, go to www.heinemann.co.uk/hotlinks (express code 4240P) and follow the links for 'Inter-Faith Network', 'Church Action on Poverty', 'CAFOD', or 'Christian Aid'.

For discussion

'All Christians need to do is love their neighbour for the world to be a better place.' Do you agree?

Summary

- Christians work for community cohesion in a variety of ways, by not being prejudiced or discriminating against others in their community and supporting groups that work for justice and fairness.
- Christians believe it is important to follow Jesus's example and teachings by helping to bring about harmonious relationships between different groups of people in society.

4.5 The Ten Commandments as a guide for living

Learning outcomes

By the end of this lesson you should be able to:

● state what the Ten Commandments are

● give your own opinion, with reasons, about the Ten Commandments as a guide for living

● explain how and why Christians use the Ten Commandments as a guide for living

● evaluate the importance of the Ten Commandments as a guide for living.

Activities

1 To help you learn the Ten Commandments, write them out in your own words and draw a symbol by each.

2 In groups, each take two of the commandments and prepare a presentation for the rest of the group on why your two commandments are still important and relevant for Christians today.

What are the Ten Commandments?

The Ten Commandments are found in the Old Testament (see page 34). The first five books in the Bible contain many commandments given by God to Moses. Christians today believe these ten are the most important. The Ten Commandments can be divided into two – those that show respect for God and those that show respect for others.

RESPECT FOR GOD

HAVE NO OTHER GODS BEFORE ME

DO NOT MAKE A CARVED IMAGE

DO NOT MISUSE GOD'S NAME

KEEP THE SABBATH DAY HOLY

RESPECT FOR OTHERS

HONOUR YOUR MOTHER AND FATHER

DO NOT COMMIT MURDER

DO NOT COMMIT ADULTERY

DO NOT STEAL

DO NOT BEAR FALSE WITNESS

DO NOT COVET

For discussion

● Catholics say the commandments were written by 'the finger of God'. What do you think this means?

● 'The Commandments are no longer relevant in the 21st century.' Do you agree?

Sacred texts

'The Ten Commandments' (Exodus 20:1–17; Deuteronomy 5:6–21)

Following the Ten Commandments today

1 God is the most important thing over everything else. This is as important today as it was at the time of Moses.

2 Today Christians take this to mean that other things can become idols or be worshipped, such as the love of money or fame. Christians should not value material things or people more than God.

3 God's name should only be used in worship. Making a promise in God's name must be kept.

4 God is worthy of praise and devotion, and the Sabbath – Sunday for Christians – should be kept as a special time.

5 Showing respect to parents allows them to carry out their parental responsibilities and ensures a strong family. As God is seen as the Father (see pages 6–7), by respecting one's parents a Christian is also showing respect for God.

6 As Christians believe all human life is a gift from God, no one except God has the right to take it away. Therefore murder is wrong. Many Christians take this to mean that such things as abortion, euthanasia and capital punishment are also wrong.

7 Adultery is wrong because it is a threat to marriage and family life, which Christians believe is very important for living a good life.

8 Taking things that are not yours – stealing – shows lack of respect for others and their property. In today's world this can also mean non-payment of debts and cheating people out of money.

9 People should not lie, spread rumours or gossip about others. Christians must stand by the truth of Christianity and live a life that values the truth in all things.

10 Christians should not be jealous of the things other people have. Envy can lead to stealing or adultery. By guarding against jealously, Christians are avoiding greed and the love of money.

ResultsPlus
Watch out!

Some candidates incorrectly give the Golden Rule as one of the Ten Commandments.

101

How the commandments help Christians to live good lives

Jesus taught that the Greatest Commandments were to love God, and to love others. The first four commandments tell Christians how they can show love for God. The next six show how Christians can love others.

As these rules come from God, and are not made by humans, they are important in guiding Christians in how they should respond to issues in the world today. For example, when it comes to making laws on such issues as abortion and freedom of the press.

Activities

Challenge

3 Christian traditions number the commandments slightly differently. List the Ten Commandments as used by Catholic Christians. How are they different from the list we have looked at here?

Summary

- The first four commandments tell Christians that they must put God first in their lives.

- The last six commandments tell Christians how they can show their love for others.

- The commandments are important to Christians because they believe they come from God.

- The commandments give Christians a guide on how to live a good life today.

4.6 The Sermon on the Mount and the Law of Moses

102

Learning outcomes

By the end of this lesson, you should be able to:

- describe how Jesus reinterpreted the Law of Moses in the Sermon on the Mount
- give your own opinion, with a reason, about Jesus's reinterpretation of the Law of Moses
- explain the meaning of Jesus's teachings about the reinterpretation of the Law of Moses
- evaluate Jesus's teachings about the reinterpretation of the Law of Moses.

edexcel ⠿ key terms

The Law of Moses – The laws God gave to Moses in the Old Testament.

The Sermon on the Mount – Jesus's description of Christian living.

Sacred texts

'The Sermon on the Mount' (Matthew 5:17–48)

'Jesus throws the traders out of the Temple' (Matthew 21:12–13)

Do not think that I have come to abolish the Law of Moses or the Prophets. I have not come to abolish them, but to fulfill them.

The Sermon on the Mount

The main teachings of Jesus about how to live a Christian life are found in the **Sermon on the Mount**. These teachings are found in Matthew's Gospel, in Chapters 5 to 7. The sermon includes teachings on the giving of charity, prayer, fasting, money and judgement. It is in this sermon that the Golden Rule (see pages 104–105), a key Christian teaching, is found.

Activities

1 In groups, decide on five pieces of advice you would give to a Christian as a guide for living. Which one do you think is the most important? Why?

For discussion

In the Sermon on the Mount Jesus said he had come to fulfil the law. What do you think he meant by this? Why do you think laws need reinterpreting? Can you think of examples of laws in this country that have changed?

For discussion

Do you think it is possible to 'turn the other cheek' all the time?

The Law of Moses

The **Law of Moses** is the term for the laws given by God that are found in the Old Testament. As a Jew, Jesus would have been required to follow these laws. Jesus reinterpreted these laws for his followers and today Christians use them as a guide for living. Jesus referred to some of these old laws and explained that his followers needed to do more than these laws asked of them – for example, they should not get angry, and they should turn the other cheek and pray for their enemies. These things would have been very difficult for people to accept in Jesus's time.

Jesus (on the right) made clear the laws that Moses (on the left) created thousands of years earlier.

What do Christians learn from these teachings?

Jesus taught that a person's thoughts and feelings are what matters. Murder starts with anger and hating someone. Adultery starts with lustful thoughts about someone other than your partner. Jesus said it was the thoughts and feelings that are the start of sinful actions. We therefore need to be careful about what we think and feel.

Jesus taught that we should not seek revenge or want to get our own back on someone who has done us wrong. We should respond to evil acts by doing good. This way a Christian is following the teachings of Jesus and setting a good Christian example.

It is the spirit of the law rather than the letter that is important. At the time of Jesus some believed a man could get a divorce if his wife displeased him in some way. Jesus made it clear that the spirit of this law was to allow divorce only if adultery had been committed.

Activities

2 Make a table of Jesus's teachings and how Christians can use these teachings in their lives today.

Challenge

3 How do Jesus's teachings about the reinterpretation of the Law of Moses help a Christian to respond to the following issues?

- punishment of criminals
- fighting in a war
- speaking out about injustices in the world.

For discussion

Did Jesus go against his own teachings when he got angry and threw the traders out of the temple in Jerusalem during the last week of his life?

Summary

- The Sermon on the Mount gives the teachings of Jesus on how Christians should live their lives.
- Jesus reinterpreted the Law of Moses and said that people should not get angry, seek revenge, or make oaths.
- Jesus said people's thoughts and feelings were as important as their actions.

4.7 The Sermon on the Mount and displaying religion

Learning outcomes

By the end of this lesson, you should be able to:

- describe the teachings about displaying religion from the Sermon on the Mount
- give your own opinion, with a reason, about displaying religion
- explain the meaning of Jesus's teachings about displaying religion
- evaluate Jesus' teachings about displaying religion.

edexcel ⠿ key terms

Displaying religion – Making a show of your religion, e.g. by praying in the street.

Hypocrite – A person who acts in a way that contradicts what they say.

Charity – Voluntary giving to those in need.

Sacred texts

'Displaying religion' (Matthew 6:1–18)

In what ways is the person in the picture a hypocrite?

Making a show of religion

In the Sermon on the Mount Jesus talked about three ways a person can show their religion by giving to **charity**, prayer and fasting

Jesus said that if people made a public display of doing these things (**displaying religion**), then they were doing so to show off to others and make themselves look good, rather than to please God. By making a public display of worshipping God, you are doing it so that others think you are a good person and not to please God; this means you are a **hypocrite**.

What Jesus said about displaying religion

Prayer

There were some religious groups at the time of Jesus whose custom was to pray openly in public places, and say long prayers, so that other people would see them and think they were truly good and religious. Jesus taught that sincere prayers should be short and directed quietly to God.

Fasting

At the time of Jesus, fasting was seen as a religious duty. Jesus did not disagree with this, but he objected to those who drew attention to themselves when they fasted, to earn the praise of their fellow men rather than to please God.

Charity

At the time of Jesus, it was considered an important religious duty to give to the needy. It was the custom to announce you had done this by blowing a trumpet. Jesus taught this was wrong and the only gifts that mattered to God were those given in secret.

Activities

1 In pairs, find three examples of how people can be hypocritical today.

2 Summarise what Jesus taught in the Sermon on the Mount about displaying religion.

Activities

Challenge

3 Read The Lord's Prayer in Matthew 6:9–13 and explain why it is described as the model Christian prayer.

To find out more about the Lord's Prayer, go to www.heinemann.co.uk/hotlinks (express code 4240P, link to 'Lord's Prayer').

For discussion

'As long as charity is given, it does not matter how it is given.' Do you agree?

For discussion

- What is prayer? How is this person following the teachings of Jesus?
- 'As long you do the right thing, the reason does not matter.' Do you agree?

Giving to charity today

Jesus taught that Christians should love their neighbour. One way of showing this is by giving to charity to help those in need. Jesus makes it very clear in his teaching that a Christian's motivation should be to help others, because this is what God wants them to do, and not to get praise and recognition from others. When Christians give to charity today, they believe it should be done privately, and without publicising the fact. This way they will receive praise from God.

Praying and fasting today.

Jesus criticises those who make a show of their religion. Therefore, when praying and fasting, Christians should do so privately and without making a show. It is important that prayers are directed to God. Jesus said that prayers should be short and he gives the example of 'The Lord's Prayer' (Our Father).

Today, the Lord's Prayer is the most important prayer for Christians. It is the ideal model for prayer, as it includes adoration, confession and petition.

Activities

4 Imagine you are a vicar and you are concerned that the people in your parish are making a display of their religion. You decide to write an article in the parish magazine, to help your parishioners understand what Jesus taught about this. Write the article.

Summary

- Jesus taught that displaying religion is wrong. The giving of charity, praying and fasting should be done privately and quietly so that it is known only to God.
- Displaying religion makes a Christian hypocritical because they are doing it to seek the approval of others and not in a sincere way to please God.

4.8 The Sermon on the Mount and money

106

Spiritual versus material wealth

Jesus taught that spiritual wealth, such as loving God and others, lasts forever. Material wealth such as big houses, fast cars and expensive clothes do not last forever. Material things are temporary. They can be eaten by moths, attacked by rust or stolen by others. Spiritual treasures cannot be destroyed or stolen, and if they are valued, the reward will come in Heaven.

God versus money

Jesus said you cannot serve two masters, both God and money. If people value money too highly, and believe it can bring happiness, then they are in danger of making it into a god. This means they will do anything for money and can become selfish. Money can become an idol that is worshipped rather than God. Jesus taught that God must be put first, above all other things.

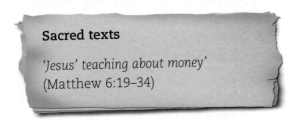

Every week millions of people enter the National Lottery draw. Why do you think they do this?

Sacred texts

'Jesus' teaching about money' (Matthew 6:19–34)

Activities

1 In groups, devise a short drama piece on the theme of spiritual wealth versus material wealth.

ResultsPlus
Watch out!

When asked about what the Sermon on the Mount teaches, many candidates refer to other teachings not found in the Sermon on the Mount, and so gain no marks.

For discussion

'Money is the root of all evil.' Do you agree?

In Matthew 19:24 Jesus said it is easier for a camel to go through the eye of a needle than for a rich man to enter the Kingdom of God. What do you think he meant?

God will provide

Jesus taught people that they should not worry about the future, as God will always provide what they need. God provides wild animals with what they need to live, and wild flowers always look beautiful. God will always provide for those that love him. Christians believe it is important for them to focus on loving God and each other rather than worry about material things, as God will always provide for them.

For discussion

John Wesley (the founder of the Methodist Church) said 'Make all you can, Save all you can, Give all you can.' Do you agree with this? Do you think it follows the teaching about money in the Sermon on the Mount?

Sacred texts

'The story of the rich young man' (Matthew 19:16–30)

Activities

Challenge

4 Read the story of the rich young man. What does it teach Christians today about the dangers of money?

The importance of Jesus's teaching on money

It helps Christians to understand the value of money in the world today. Even though money is necessary, it should not become more important than loving God and others.

It shows Christians that they can become easily distracted by money. Money should be the servant, not the master, and used for God's purposes, not as an end in itself.

Christians should not worry about money and possessions. They should trust that God will provide for their needs.

If Christians spend all their time making money this will stop them spending time with God or serving God.

Activities

2 Find out about a wealthy Christian who has followed the teaching about money in the Sermon on the Mount.

3 A Christian wins a lot of money and writes to you for advice on what to do. What advice would you give? Write a letter in reply.

For discussion

Can you be rich at the same time as being a Christian?

Summary

- Jesus said you cannot serve money and God.
- Spiritual treasures such as the love of God and others will last forever.
- Material treasures will be taken from you and do not last forever.
- Christians should not worry about money, as God will provide for them.

4.9 The Sermon on the Mount and judgement

108

For discussion

When Madonna adopted 13-month-old David from Malawi in 2006, many people criticised her for doing so. Do you think people were right to judge her in this way?

What is judgement?

Judgement is the act of forming an opinion about someone or something. We make judgements about many things – what we like and dislike, what is important to us, what we think about others and their actions.

When we judge other people and their actions we are saying we agree or disagree with them. What right do Christians have to judge other people, and on what basis can they do this?

What the Sermon on the Mount teaches Christians about judgement.

● We should not judge other people.
● If we judge someone, then we must expect to be judged in the same way.
● We should judge ourselves before we judge others.
● The most important thing is try to make yourself a good Christian before you criticise the behaviour and actions of other people.

Sacred texts

'Judging others' (Matthew 7:1–6)

Activities

1 Read Matthew 7:1–6. Create four PowerPoint® slides to explain what Jesus taught about judgement.

For discussion

'Judging others is a natural thing to do, therefore it cannot be wrong.' Do you agree?

Prejudice starts with people making judgements about others. Prejudice is a belief that other people are inferior or superior without even knowing them, and making a judgement about them. This leads to discrimination against groups of people because of such things as colour, background, lifestyle and religion, which Christians know is wrong.

A key Christian teaching is to love others. This means accepting people as they are and not making judgements about them. Knowing that you will be judged in the same way you judge other people makes people more sensitive to the needs of others.

Christians need to separate the action from the person. The action may be bad or evil, but not the person. Only God can judge others. This means they should speak out against injustices but not judge the person. It is the sin that is hated, not the sinner.

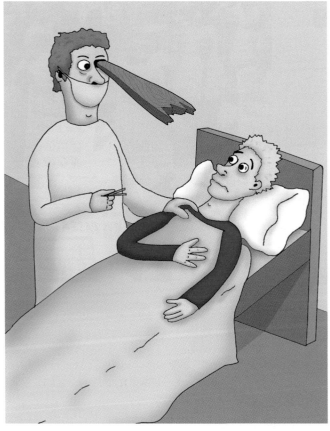

Jesus uses the analogy of a plank and sawdust when teaching about judging others. What point do you think Jesus was trying to make?

The importance of Jesus's teachings about judgement for Christians today

Jesus points out that if we are quick to judge others we are forgetting we are human ourselves, and that we will also be judged. Only those who have never done anything wrong themselves should judge others. Christians should think about their own faults, and put these right first before passing judgement on others.

Gossip is a way of judging others. Gossip can hurt other people so should be avoided. This is important for Christians today, as we live in a world that thrives on gossip – it is seen daily in the newspapers, magazines and on television.

Activities

2 Explain how Christians today should use the teachings about judgement in the Sermon on the Mount as a guide for living.

Challenge

3 'Without judgement there cannot be justice'. Explain, with examples, what you think this means. Do you agree? Give your reasons.

Summary

- Jesus teaches that judging others is wrong.
- Christians should judge themselves first, before making judgements about others.
- Christians should remember that if they judge others, they too will be judged in the same way.

4.10 The Golden Rule

Learning outcomes

By the end of this lesson you should be able to:

- describe the meaning of the Golden Rule
- give your own opinion, with a reason, about the Golden Rule
- explain how and why Christians use the Golden Rule as a guide for living
- evaluate the importance of the Golden Rule for Christians.

Buddhism
Treat not others in ways that you yourself would find hurtful.

Islam
Not one of you truly believes until you wish for others what you wish for yourself.

Hinduism
This is the sum of duty: do not do to others what would cause pain if done to you.

The Golden Rule

Christianity
Do to others what you would have them do to you, for this sums up the Law and the Prophets.

Sikhism
I am a stranger to no one; and no one is a stranger to me. Indeed, I am a friend to all.

Judaism
What is hateful to you, do not do to your neighbour. This is the whole Torah; all the rest is commentary.

For discussion

Why do you think all the major world religions have a rule similar to the Golden Rule in Christianity?

Activities

1 In groups, come up with examples of when people can be seen to be following the Golden Rule and when they have not followed it. You might find it helpful to look through newspapers for examples.

Treat others as you would want to be treated

The teaching found in the Sermon on the Mount and in Luke's Gospel has become known as the Golden Rule, as it sums up how a Christian should behave towards other people. The Golden Rule can be applied to different situations and it acts as a guide for Christians. Today it is usually summarised as 'treat others as you would like them to treat you'.

Sacred texts

'The Golden Rule' (Matthew 7:12)

What the Sermon the Mount teaches about the Golden Rule

- All the teachings in the Jewish Scriptures (Old Testament) can be summed up by the Golden Rule.
- By following the Golden Rule, Christians will always treat others well because nobody wants to hurt or treat themselves badly.
- By following the Golden Rule we are likely to keep the commandment to love our neighbour.

The importance of the Golden Rule for Christians today

The Golden Rule is an easy teaching to apply to all situations in life, whether at home, school, work or leisure. Christians just need to think about how they would want to be treated if they were in the same situation and then act accordingly.

If all people followed the Golden Rule then the world would be a better place to live in. All religions have a similar teaching about how to treat others.

Christians believe they should follow the teachings of Jesus. Therefore, following the Golden Rule is central to being a Christian, as Jesus said it summed up all other teachings.

The Golden Rule is just as important to follow when it comes to big moral and social issues as it is for dealing with other people in our everyday lives. It can act as a guide for governments when deciding such issues as the role of prisons, asylum seekers, and the care of the elderly in society.

For discussion

The civil rights movement in America during the 1960s demanded equal rights for black Americans. In June 1963 two young black people went to enrol at the University of Alabama but were prevented. President J F Kennedy intervened and they were allowed to enrol. The same evening, the President broadcast to the nation about the day's events. He said, 'The heart of the question is whether all Americans are to be afforded equal rights and equal opportunities, whether we are going to treat our fellow Americans as we want to be treated.' Why do you think he made reference to the Golden Rule in his speech?

Activities

2 In groups, plan an assembly for Year 7 on how the Golden Rule can be applied to modern-day moral issues. You may want to produce a short sketch or play, use role-play or a PowerPoint® presentation to make your points clear to your audience.

ResultsPlus
Build better answers

Explain why many Christians use the Sermon on the Mount as a basis for living the Christian life. (8 marks)

 Basic, 1–2-mark answer
A brief reason given or description of the issue.

 Good, 3–4-mark answer
Two brief reasons or a developed reason.

 Excellent, 7–8-mark answer
Four brief reasons, two developed reasons, three reasons with one developed, or comprehensive explanation.

Summary

- The Golden Rule teaches Christians that they should always treat others as they wish to be treated themselves.
- The Golden Rule is a summary of the teachings found in the Jewish Scriptures.
- Through following the Golden Rule, Christians are keeping the commandment to love their neighbour.

4.11 The relief of poverty and suffering in the UK

Learning outcomes

By the end of this lesson you should be able to:

- describe what the Salvation Army does to help others in the UK
- give your own opinion, with reasons, about the work of the Salvation Army
- explain how the Salvation Army helps to relieve poverty and suffering
- evaluate the work of the Salvation Army in relieving poverty and suffering.

The work of the Salvation Army today

The work of the Salvation Army includes:

- helping the homeless
- caring for children and families
- working with young people
- care for the elderly
- helping in emergencies
- campaigning about social and moral issues.

This is the first slide from a presentation about the Salvation Army. From what you can see on this slide, make a list of the activities the Salvation Army do and how they help other people.

Activities

1 In groups, choose one of the ways the Salvation Army helps to relieve poverty and suffering. Find out how they help. Report your findings back to the class.

2 Invite a member of the Salvation Army into school to talk about their work, or watch a DVD produced by the Salvation Army. Write a summary of the work they do, with the title 'Belief in Action'.

To find out more about how the Salvation Army helps to relieve poverty and suffering in the UK, go to www.heinemann.co.uk/hotlinks (express code 4240P, link to 'Salvation Army').

The Salvation Army

In the UK there are over 800 Salvation Army parishes and 54,000 members. It was started in 1865 in the East End of London by William Booth, a Christian who wanted to preach the Gospel but also help the poor. Today, the Salvation Army is known for its work with people who have fallen on hard times for a variety of reasons.

For discussion

'No one is really poor in the UK today.'
Do you agree?

Salvation Army objects to Super Casino

A bid to build a Las Vegas style casino in Middlesbrough is opposed by the Salvation Army. A representative from the Salvation Army said; 'We are against this, not from a religious viewpoint, but for the impact it will have on people's social wellbeing. We are heavily involved in working with people, especially in the areas of poverty and addiction. Based on our experience in these areas, we believe the casino will have a negative impact upon the people of Middlesbrough.'

(Adapted from BBC News Online)

For discussion

- Read the news article. Why do you think the Salvation Army objected to the building of the casino? Do you think they were right to do so?
- William Booth said he believed in 'soup, soap and salvation.' What do you think he meant by this? Does it still apply to the UK today?

Helping the homeless

The Salvation Army run hostels that offer safe temporary accommodation and help people to develop skills that will give them the ability to provide for themselves.

For those who live rough on the streets, the Salvation Army provides soup kitchens, clothing and blankets. Drop-in centres provide a place where homeless people can meet others and can access support services such as medical help.

Helping in emergencies

The Salvation Army aims to relieve distress and suffering wherever it is found. In 2007, it responded to 202 different incidents including the floods in Yorkshire. On 7 July 2005, after the terrorist attacks on London, the Salvation Army were there supporting the emergency services and helping the victims. The support they offer includes providing refreshments and emotional support at the incident site and support for families, many of whom might have suffered bereavement.

Human trafficking

The Salvation Army responds to modern-day issues such as human trafficking. Their work focuses on three areas:

- education and campaigning
- fundraising
- provision of care.

The Salvation Army provides emergency accommodation and safe houses for the victims of human trafficking. Since 2004 the Salvation Army has actively worked to raise awareness of the issue and works with other groups and the government in combating human trafficking.

Activities

Challenge

3 There are many other Christian organisations that work to relieve poverty and suffering in the UK. Find out about the work of one and compare it with the work of the Salvation Army. A good example is the Catholic charity, the St Vincent de Paul Society (SVP).

Find out more about the St Vincent de Paul Society, another Christian organisation in the UK that works to help those in need, by going to www.heinemann.co.uk/hotlinks (express code 4240P).

Summary

- The Salvation Army works to relieve poverty and suffering in the UK.
- The Salvation Army is known for its work with the homeless, families facing difficulties, and support for people during emergencies.

4.12 Why Christians work to relieve poverty and suffering

Learning outcomes

By the end of this lesson you should be able to:

● give your own opinion, with reasons, about why the Salvation Army works to relieve poverty and suffering

● explain why the Salvation Army helps to relieve poverty and suffering

● evaluate the work of the Salvation Army in relieving poverty and suffering.

Sacred texts

'Levi is called to be a disciple' (Mark 2:13–17)

'The Son of Man came to serve' (Mark 10:45)

'The Greatest Commandment' (Mark 12:29–31)

Causes of poverty

- Poor mental or physical health
- Homelessness
- Poor education
- Following the example of Jesus
- Unemployment
- Addictions – alcohol, drugs, gambling

The Salvation Army started working in the East End of London in the late 19th century, where many people lived in extreme poverty.

Activities

1 Illustrate the causes of poverty with drawings or cuttings from magazines and newspapers.

Christian values

To lead a good Christian life, Christians are required to show Christian values. These values are the things that Jesus himself did or taught:

● Jesus helped others
● Jesus healed the sick
● Jesus mixed with the outcasts of society and made them feel valued
● in the parable of the Good Samaritan (see pages 18–19), Jesus taught that loving your neighbour means showing compassion for all people
● in the parable of the Sheep and the Goats (see page 20), Jesus taught that, through helping the hungry and homeless, Christians are helping Jesus himself
● the Golden Rule (see pages 110–111) teaches that Christians should treat others as they would like to be treated
● Jesus said that he had come to serve and not to be served; Christians should do likewise
● Jesus taught that the Greatest Commandment was to love God and others; love of others means showing concern and compassion for them.

The Salvation Army believes that doing good deeds is an essential part of being a Christian. These people are having breakfast at a Salvation Army residential centre.

Faith in action

For members of the Salvation Army, faith without action is worthless. Helping others is an essential part of faith. The teachings and actions of Jesus make that clear. Members of the Salvation Army also show concern for the causes of poverty, and work against the injustices in society that cause suffering and hardship.

Faith and action go hand in hand. The Letter of James says that faith that does not lead to good deeds is dead, and asks how it is possible to prove you have faith without doing good to others. Having faith is the way to salvation and eternal life in Heaven.

Helping others is a way the Salvation Army can show their faith. It is through their actions, and often through loving people who are hard to love, that others may come to understand and accept the message of Christianity.

Activities

Challenge

2 In 2004 The Salvation Army founded ALOVE, a group for young people. Find out why they gave it this name.

Seeking justice for all

The Salvation Army speaks out against injustices in society. They offer advice to the government on various issues such as homelessness and gambling. Recently they have been working to raise the issue of human trafficking.

The Bible teaches that God is a God of justice. All Christians should behave justly to others and work for justice for all people. In Amos, a book in the Old Testament, we are told of God's anger at the people who did nothing to help the poor and denied justice to the oppressed.

Sacred texts

'Faith and deeds' (James 2:14–19)

'Justice for the poor and oppressed' (Amos 5:21–24; 8:4–6)

Activities

3 Explain the reasons why a Christian organisation works to relieve poverty and suffering in the UK.

For discussion

- 'Poverty is the responsibility of the government, not religion.' Do you agree?
- 'Everyone has the right to the basic necessities of life'. What are they? Do you agree?

Summary

- Jesus taught that Christians have a duty to help the poor and those who are suffering.
- By helping the poor and those who are suffering Christians are following the example of Jesus.
- The way to gain eternal life is through helping those who are less fortunate than you.

Quick quiz

1 Give three ways a Christian can show their vocation.

2 What are the evangelical counsels?

3 What is the difference between the active and contemplative life?

4 Give two commandments that show respect for God.

5 Give two commandments that show respect for others.

6 How did Jesus reinterpret the Law of Moses that said 'an eye for an eye and a tooth for a tooth'?

7 Which three things did Jesus talk about when teaching about displaying religion in the Sermon on the Mount?

8 Give two reasons why the teachings about money found in the Sermon on the Mount are important for Christians today.

9 What is the Golden Rule?

10 What does the analogy of the plank and speck of sawdust teach Christians about judgement?

Plenary activities

1 Design an ideas map to summarise all the different ways Christians can show their vocation.

2 In groups, make up a set of Mastermind-style questions where the specialist subject is 'The teachings in the Sermon on the Mount'. Then challenge the other teams to answer your questions.

3 Make up a mnemonic (a word or phrase) or rhyme to help you remember the Ten Commandments.

4 Hot-seating: Choose a person in the group to be in the 'hot-seat'. They have to take on the role given to them and answer all the questions you ask them. Before your start, you will need to decide the role and the topics (based on what you have learned in this section) you will be asking questions on.

Student tip

- Vocation for Christians is more than just a job.

- Remember that many Christians show their vocation in their daily life – they don't have to become a monk, nun or priest.

- Use teachings from the New Testament to explain why Christians work for social and community cohesion, for example, the parable of the Good Samaritan and Peter's vision in Acts.

- Make sure you know all of the Ten Commandments so you can use them to explain how they are used as a guide for living.

- You will need to know the key passages from the Sermon on the Mount (given in the specification).

- Remember – you need to know the three ways Jesus taught that religion can be displayed; charity, prayer and fasting.

- Remember, when Jesus was talking about judgement in the Sermon on the Mount he was referring to how we make judgements in our lives, and not just about being judged by someone in a court of law for doing wrong.

- Don't confuse the Golden Rule with the Greatest Commandment!

- You must always name the organisation you are writing about. Make sure it is a Christian organisation working in the UK.

Self-evaluation checklist

Read through the following list and evaluate how well you know and understand each of the topics.
How well have you understood the topics in this section? In the first column of the table below use the following code to rate your understanding:

Green – I understand this fully

Orange – I am confident I can answer most questions on this

Red – I need to do a lot more work on this topic.

In the second and third columns you need to think about:

◗ Whether you have an opinion on this topic and could give reasons for that opinion if asked

◗ Whether you can give the opinion of someone who disagrees with you and give reasons for this alternative opinion.

Content covered	My understanding is red/orange/green	Can I give my opinion?	Can I give an alternative opinion?
◗ The meaning of vocation and its importance for Christians.			
◗ How and why Christians show vocation in their daily life and how and why some Christians take holy orders.			
◗ How and why some Christians are involved in working for social and community cohesion.			
◗ How and why Christians use the Ten Commandments as a guide for living.			
◗ How and why Christians use the reinterpretation of the Law of Moses in the Sermon on the Mount on displaying religion, money, judgement and the Golden Rule as a guide for living.			
◗ How and why one Christian organisation helps to relieve poverty/ suffering in the UK.			

Find out more

- To find out more about Christian vocations, go to www.heinemann.co.uk/hotlinks (express code 4240P) and follow the link for 'Christian vocations'.
- Look out for newspaper articles or items in the news about the work people are doing for social and community cohesion.
- Invite some people from your local Christian community into school, and ask them how they follow the Ten Commandments and the Sermon on the Mount in their daily lives.
- Church Action on Poverty is a Christian organisation that works to relieve poverty in the UK. You can find out more about their work, go to www.heinemann.co.uk/hotlinks (express code 4240P, link 'Church Action on Poverty').

Know Zone
Section 4: Living the Christian life

Remember to use the marks given for each part of a question as a guide as to how much time you should spend on them.

You do not have to work through the sections. You can answer the sections in any order.

You must answer all the parts of the question you choose. You must not answer (a) from one question and (b) from another and so on.

Make sure you read the key term (in bold type) carefully so that you give the correct meaning.

The question asks you to explain how you connect the two ideas in the question. In this question you need to say what the organisation does to help stop poverty.

Mini Exam Paper

(a) What is **contemplative life**? (2 marks)

(b) Should people make a display of their religion?

Give two reasons for your point of view. (4 marks)

(c) Explain how one Christian organisation works to end poverty and/or suffering in the UK. (8 marks)

(d) 'People cannot serve God and money.' In your answer you should refer to Christianity.

(i) Do you agree? Give reasons for your opinion. (3 marks)

(ii) Give reason why some people might disagree with you. (3 marks)

Make sure the reasons you give are developed.

You must refer to Christianity in either (i) or (ii) otherwise you cannot get more than three marks for the whole question.

If a question asks for the teachings from the Sermon on the Mount, make sure you do not include other teachings.

Support activities

1 Here are some sample (b)-type questions. Practise by answering these, giving developed reasons for agreeing and disagreeing.

- Should people show more respect for God? Give two reasons for your point of view.

- Do you think judging others is wrong? Give two reasons for your point of view.

(d) 'People cannot serve God and money.'

In your answer you should refer to Christianity.

(i) Do you agree? Give reasons for your opinion. (3 marks)

(ii) Give reasons why some people might disagree with you. (3 marks)

Student answer

(i) I agree you can serve God and money as you can give money to charity, which is serving God. Many rich people go to church and worship God, so are serving God.

(ii) Some people will disagree because Jesus said in the Sermon on the Mount that you cannot serve God and money.

Examiner comments

The candidate has referred to Christianity so can get maximum marks.

In (i) the candidate has given two simple reasons for their point of view.

It would be given 2 marks.

In (ii) The candidate has given one simple reason.

It would be given 1 mark.

Build a better answer

I agree you can serve God and money as you can give money to charity, which is serving God. If you make a lot of money, for example, you can use it to support the work of Christian Aid, which helps children in developing countries who are part of God's creation. Also, many rich people go to church and worship God, so they are serving God.

(ii) Some people will disagree because Jesus said in the Sermon on the Mount that you cannot serve God and money. For some people money is the most important thing. They become greedy and do not follow what God wants them to do. If money is so important to you, you will spend all your time making more and have no time left to worship God.

Welcome to examzone

Revising for your exams can be a daunting prospect. In this part of the book we'll take you through the best way of revising for your exams, step by step, to ensure you get the best results possible.

Zone In!

Have you ever become so absorbed in a task that suddenly it feels entirely natural and easy to perform? This is a feeling familiar to many athletes and performers. They work hard to recreate it in competition in order to do their very best. It's a feeling of being 'in the zone', and if you can achieve that same feeling in an examination, the chances are you'll perform brilliantly.

The good news is that you can get 'in the zone' by taking some simple steps in advance of the exam. Here are our top tips.

UNDERSTAND IT

Make sure you understand the exam process and what revision you need to do. This will give you confidence and also help you to get things into proportion. These pages are a good place to find some starting pointers for performing well in exams.

FRIENDS AND FAMILY

Make sure that your friends and family know when you want to revise. Even share your revision plan with them. Learn to control your times with them, so you don't get distracted. This means you can have better quality time with them when you aren't revising, because you aren't worrying about what you ought to be doing.

DEAL WITH DISTRACTIONS

Think about the issues in your life that may interfere with revision. Write them all down. Then think about how you can deal with each so they don't affect your revision.

COMPARTMENTALISE

You might not be able to deal with all the issues that can distract you. For example, you may be worried about a friend who is ill, or just be afraid of the exam. In this case, there is still a useful technique you can use. Put all of these worries into an imagined box in your mind at the start of your revision (or in the exam) and mentally lock it. Only open it again at the end of your revision session (or exam).

DIET AND EXERCISE

Make sure you eat sensibly and exercise as well! If your body is not in the right state, how can your mind be? A substantial breakfast will set you up for the day, and a light evening meal will keep your energy levels high.

BUILD CONFIDENCE

Use your revision time not only to revise content, but also to build your confidence in readiness for tackling the examination. For example, try tackling a short sequence of easy tasks in record time.

Planning Zone

The key to success in exams and revision often lies in good planning. Knowing **what** you need to do and **when** you need to do it is your best path to a stress-free experience. Here are some top tips in creating a great personal revision plan.

First of all, *know your strengths and weaknesses.*

Go through each topic making a list of how well you think you know the topic. Use your mock examination results and/or any other test results that are available as a check on your self-assessment. This will help you to plan your personal revision effectively, putting extra time into your weaker areas.

Next, *create your plan!*

Remember to make time for considering how topics interrelate.

For example, in PE you will be expected to know not just about the various muscles, but how these relate to various body types.

The specification quite clearly states when you are expected to be able to link one topic to another so plan this into your revision sessions.

You will be tested on this in the exam and you can gain valuable marks by showing your ability to do this.

Finally, *follow the plan!*

You can use the revision sections in the following pages to kick-start your revision.

MAY

SUNDAY	MONDAY	TUESI
29	30	1

Be realistic about how much time you can devote to your revision, but also make sure you put in enough time. Give yourself regular breaks or different activities to give your life some variance. Revision need not be a prison sentence!

Find out your exam dates. Go to the Edexcel website **www.edexcel.com** to find all final exam dates, and check with your teacher.

view Sectio
complete t
ractice exa
question

Chunk your revision in each subject down into smaller sections. This will make it more manageable and less daunting.

Draw up a list of all the dates from the start of your revision right through to your exams.

13

Review Sectio
Complete three
practice exam

20

Review Sectio
Try the Keywor
Quiz again

Make sure you allow time for assessing your progress against your initial self-assessment. Measuring progress will allow you to see and be encouraged by your improvement. These little victories will build your confidence.

22

EXAM DAY!

27

28

29

Know Zone
Section 1: Beliefs and values

In this section you'll find some useful suggestions about how to structure your revision for each of the main topics. You might want to read through this before starting your revision planning, to help you think about the best way to revise what you've learnt. Remember, different people learn in different ways – some remember *visually* and therefore might want to think about using diagrams and other drawings for their revision, whereas others remember better through *sound* or through *writing things out*. Some people work best alone, whereas others work best when bouncing ideas off friends on the same course.

Revision

Look back at the KnowZone on pages 28–29. Read through the Self-evaluation checklist and think about which are your stronger and weaker areas, so that you can focus on the ones you are less confident about. The support activities below are designed to help you revise this section.

When you are ready for some exam practice, read through the KnowZone on pages 30–31. Then you might like to attempt the questions below.

Practice exam questions

(a) What is **monotheism**? (2 marks)

(b) Should God be described as Father? Give **two** reasons for your point of view. (4 marks)

(c) Explain why Christians believe in the Trinity? (8 marks)

(d) 'The Holy Spirit is active in the world today.' In your answer you should refer to Christianity.

  (i) Do you agree? Give reasons for your opinion. (3 marks)

  (ii) Give reasons why some people may disagree with you (3 marks)

Support activities

KEY TERMS

1 For the key terms for this section design a set of revision cards. You need 12 pieces of card about the size of postcards. For each key term write the definition, and draw a symbol or image that will help you remember it.

BELIEFS

God as Unity

Jesus as the Son of God

God as the Trinity

God as the Father

Christian beliefs

God as the Creator

The Holy Spirit

Salvation from sin

2 In groups, challenge each other to talk for a minute about one of the topics on the spidergram without repeating or hesitating.

VALUES

You will be examined on your understanding about the importance of the **love of God** and **love of others** and how this love is shown.

3 (a) Design an ideas map for 'The love of God' and for 'The love of others'.

Or

   (b) As a group or a class, each give one piece of information about love of God or love of others, then the next person has to repeat it and add one of their own and so on around the group or class. See how many you can remember as a group.

Know Zone
Section 2: Community and tradition

Revision

Look back at the KnowZone on pages 56–57. Read through the self-evaluation checklist and think about which are your stronger and weaker areas, so that you can focus on the ones you are less confident about. The support activities below are designed to help you revise this section.

When you are ready for some exam practice, read through the KnowZone on pages 58–59. Then you might like to attempt the questions below.

Practice exam questions

(a) Who are the **laity**? (2 marks)

(b) Do you think the Bible is important today?

Give **two** reasons for your point of view. (4 marks)

(c) Explain the importance of Apostolic succession for Catholic Christians. (8 marks)

(d) 'The Church does not need bishops.' In your answer you should refer to Christianity.

(i) Do you agree? Give reasons for your opinion. (3 marks)

(ii Give reasons why some people may disagree with you. (3 marks)

Support activities

1   As a class or a group, divide into two teams. One person is given a key term card. They have to mime it to their team who have a minute to guess the answer before the other team can join in and try to guess what it is.

THE BIBLE

2   Make up a revision card on the following topics to do with the Bible:
   (a) the Old Testament
   (b) the New testament
   (c) reasons for believing the Bible is the word of God
   (d) reasons for believing the Bible is inspired by the Holy Spirit
   (e) reasons for believing the Bible was written by humans
   (f) why the Bible is important
   (g) different attitudes to the authority of the Bible.

Bible as the word of God

- *Unity* in the message therefore must be one author – GOD.
- *Jesus' life and death* fulfilled the *prophecies* in the *Old Testament* therefore must be the word of God
- *Jesus said* the *Old Testament* was the *word of God*
- Many have had a *personal experience* that has lead them to believe

THE CHURCH

3   Give the different Christian viewpoints about each of the following topics:
   (a) the apostolic tradition
   (b) the authority of the Church
   (c) the Pope and bishops
   (d) the Virgin Mary
   (e) celibacy of the clergy.

THE ROLE OF THE PRIEST/MINISTER AND THE CHURCH IN THE LOCAL AREA

4   **Hot-seating**. One member of the group sits in the 'hot seat' and takes on the role of a priest. The rest of the group asks them questions about their role and the role of the church and their importance to the local area.

Know Zone
Section 3: Worship and celebration

Revision

Look back at the KnowZone on pages 86–87. Read through the self-evaluation checklist and think about which are your stronger and weaker areas, so that you can focus on the ones you are less confident about. The support activities below are designed to help you revise this section.

When you are ready for some exam practice, read through the KnowZone on pages 88–89. Then you might like to attempt the questions below.

Practice exam questions

(a) What is **believers' baptism**? (2 marks)

(b) Do you think the Eucharist is the most important form of worship?

Give **two** reasons for your point of view. (4 marks)

(c) Explain why Christians observe Holy Week. (8 marks)

(d) 'Worship is a waste of time.' In your answer you should refer to Christianity.

(i) Do you agree? Give reasons for your opinion. (3 marks)

(ii) Give reasons why some people may disagree with you. (3 marks)

Support activities

KEY TERMS

1 In pairs, on a sheet of paper draw a picture for each of the key terms for this section. Swap your sheet with another pair. Each pair has to work out what each key term is and give its definition. Check your answers with each other.

BAPTISM AND CONFIRMATION

2 For each of the following make a list or a spider diagram with ten key points:
   (a) infant baptism
   (b) adult baptism
   (c) confirmation.

THE FESTIVALS

3 In a group, choose one of the following festivals: Christmas, Lent, Holy Week and Easter. Prepare 10 questions about the festival. Now swap the questions with another group. Answer their questions and give them back for marking. You can continue to do this until you have answered questions on all the festivals.

THE EUCHARIST

4 Design an ideas map that shows the meaning and importance of the Mass or Eucharist for Christians. You need to include:
   • what happens at the Eucharist
   • what event it remembers
   • key terms linked with it
   • why it is important
   • the different beliefs about the Eucharist.

FEATURES OF A CHURCH ACTIVITY

5 Either use a game given to you by your teacher or design one yourself, to test your knowledge of the different features of the churches you have studied.

Revision

Look back at the KnowZone on pages 116–117. Read through the self-evaluation checklist and think about which are your stronger and weaker areas, so that you can focus on the ones you are less confident about. The support activities below are designed to help you revise this section.

When you are ready for some exam practice, read through the KnowZone on pages 118–119. Then you might like to attempt the questions below.

Practice exam questions

(a) What is **vocation**? (2 marks)

(b) Should people live the monastic life? Give **two** reasons for your point of view. (4 marks)

(c) Explain why many Christians use the Sermon on the Mount as a basis for living the Christian life. (8 marks)

(d) 'People should show more respect to God.' In your answer you should refer to Christianity.
   (i) Do you agree? Give reasons for your opinion. (3 marks)
   (ii) Give reasons why some people may disagree with you. (3 marks)

Support activities

1 In a table writedown each of the key terms and their definitions. Beside each key term, include a prompt to help you to remember it. This could be a simple drawing, a word, mnemonic or rhyme. You might find it helpful to group the words together in a particular order.

VOCATION

2 For each of the following make a list or a spider diagram with six key points:
   • meaning of vocation
   • vocation in daily life and work
   • holy orders.

SOCIAL AND COMMUNITY COHESION

3 Make up two revision prompt cards for social and community cohesion.
   (a) One to include the meaning of social and community cohesion and examples of the work Christians do in this area.
   (b) The other to give the reasons why Christians work for social and community cohesion.

THE TEN COMMANDMENTS

4 Design an ideas map that shows the Ten Commandments and their importance for Christians.

SERMON ON THE MOUNT

- Displaying religion
- The Law of Moses
- Money
- Sermon on the Mount teachings
- The Golden Rule
- Judgement

5 Draw another similar spider diagram and add the following information:
   • What Jesus said on each point
   • How Christians use the teaching
   • Why Christians use the teaching
   • Different points of view on the teaching.

A CHRISTIAN ORGANISATION WORKING TO RELIEVE POVERTY AND/OR SUFFERING

6 Draw up a table that shows the kinds of work done by the particular organisation you have chosen, how it relieves poverty or suffering and the reasons why it does the work.

Don't Panic Zone

As you get close to completing your revision, the Big Day will be getting nearer and nearer. Many students find this the most stressful time and tend to go into panic mode, either working long hours without really giving their brains a chance to absorb information. or giving up and staring blankly at the wall.

Panicking simply makes your brain seize up and you find that information and thoughts simply cannot flow naturally. You become distracted and anxious, and things seem worse than they are. Many students build the exams up into more than they are. Remember: the exams are not trying to catch you out! If you have studied the course, there will be no surprises on the exam paper!

Student tip
Last-minute learning tips for Religious Studies

Learn the glossary definitions for the key terms – otherwise you could lose the first two marks of each question.

In preparation for (b)-type and (d)-type questions, make a list of the reasons why people either agree or disagree with the issues or questions raised in the specification.

Make sure you are clear where there are different views amongst Christians.

Know the Bible teachings referred to in the specification and how they relate to the section being studied.

Don't panic

Exam Zone

You will have one and a half hours for this exam and in that time you have to answer **four** questions, one on each of the sections you have studied: Beliefs and values, Community and tradition, Worship and celebration, and Living the Christian life. You will be given a choice of two questions for each section.

Each question is in four parts:

- **Part (a)**: This question asks you for a definition of a word. (2 marks)

- **Part (b)**: This questions asks for your opinion on a point of view. To gain full marks you will need to give two developed reasons for your point of view. (4 marks)

- **Part (c)**: This question asks you to explain a particular belief or idea. To gain full marks you will need to give either:

  – four brief reasons with two developed reasons

  – two developed reasons

  – three reasons, one of which is developed, or

  – one fully-developed reason.

  *Don't forget that in this question the quality of your written communication will be assessed. (8 marks)

- **Part (d)**: This question is in two parts. The question will ask for your opinion on a point of view, and ask you to give an alternative point of view. You are expected to refer to Christianity in your answer. To gain full marks for each part, you need to give either:

  – three simple reasons

  – two developed reasons or

  – one fully-developed reason. (3 marks for each part)

Quality of written communication.
In each (c)-type question you can be awarded 1 mark for the quality of your written communication. That is 4 marks over the whole paper. The examiner is looking for a clear style that uses key terms, that is well organised and has very few spelling and punctuation errors.

A final point: effectively you shouldn't spend more than 22.5 minutes on each section!

Meet the exam paper

This diagram shows the front cover of the exam paper. These instructions, information and advice will always appear on the front of the paper. It is worth reading it carefully now. Check you understand it. Now is a good opportunity to ask your teacher about anything you are not sure of here.

Print your surname here, and your other names afterwards to ensure that the exam board awards the marks to the right candidate.

Here you fill in the school's exam number.

Ensure that you understand exactly how long the examination will last, and plan your time accordingly.

Note that the quality of your written communication will also be marked. Take particular care to present your thoughts and work at the highest standard you can, for maximum marks.

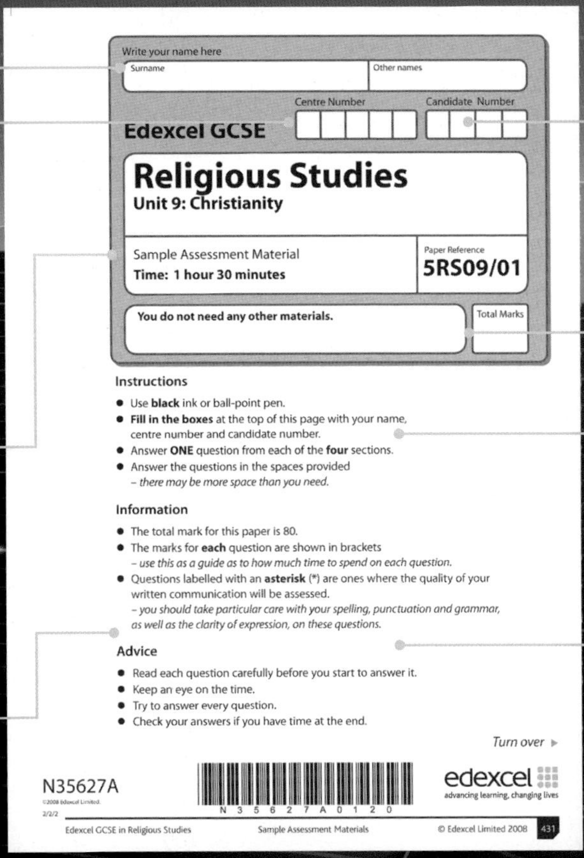

Here you fill in your personal exam number. Take care when writing it down because the number is important to the exam board when writing your score.

In this box, the examiner will write the total marks you have achieved in the exam paper.

Make sure that you understand exactly which questions from which sections you should attempt.

Don't feel that you have to fill the answer space provided. Everybody's handwriting varies, so a long answer from you may take up as much space as a short answer from someone else.

Write your name here

Surname   Other names

Centre Number   Candidate Number

Edexcel GCSE

Religious Studies
Unit 9: Christianity

Sample Assessment Material
Time: 1 hour 30 minutes

Paper Reference
5RS09/01

You do not need any other materials.

Total Marks

Instructions

- Use **black** ink or ball-point pen.
- **Fill in the boxes** at the top of this page with your name, centre number and candidate number.
- Answer **ONE** question from each of the **four** sections.
- Answer the questions in the spaces provided
  – there may be more space than you need.

Information

- The total mark for this paper is 80.
- The marks for **each** question are shown in brackets
  – use this as a guide as to how much time to spend on each question.
- Questions labelled with an **asterisk** (*) are ones where the quality of your written communication will be assessed.
  – you should take particular care with your spelling, punctuation and grammar, as well as the clarity of expression, on these questions.

Advice

- Read each question carefully before you start to answer it.
- Keep an eye on the time.
- Try to answer every question.
- Check your answers if you have time at the end.

Turn over ▶

N35627A
©2008 Edexcel Limited.
2/2/2

Edexcel GCSE in Religious Studies   Sample Assessment Materials   © Edexcel Limited 2008

edexcel
advancing learning, changing lives

431

Practical tips on the exam paper

- You must use a black pen. Your paper is scanned into a computer for marking. If you write in any other colour, you risk your work not being seen clearly.

- You must choose your question carefully – cross out the one you are not going to do – to avoid changing a question half-way through answering it. This is a very common mistake and costs candidates lots of marks!

- Mark with an x at the top of the page which question you have chosen.

- Do not write outside the guidelines – your answer may get cut off by the scanning process.

- Do not use extra sheets and attach them unless it is absolutely necessary. If you need more space – for example, for a (b) question – continue into the (c) space and when you change question write your own (c). Do the same for (c) into (d). If you then run out, put an arrow and write at the end of the exam booklet.

Zone Out

This section provides answers to the most common questions students have about what happens after they complete their exams. For more information, visit www.heinemann.co.uk/hotlinks (express code 4240P) and click on examzone.

About your grades

Whether you've done better than, worse than, or just as you expected, your grades are the final measure of your performance on your course and in the exams. On this page we explain some of the information that appears on your results slip and tell you what to do if you think something is wrong. We answer the most popular questions about grades and look at some of the options facing you.

When will my results be published?

Results for summer examinations are issued on the **middle** two Thursdays in August, with GCE first and GCSE second. November exam results are issued in January, January exam results are issued in March and March exam results are issued in April.

Can I get my results online?

Visit www.heinemann.co.uk/hotlinks (express code 4240P) and click on Results Plus, where you will find detailed student results information including the 'Edexcel Gradeometer' which demonstrates how close you were to the nearest grade boundary.

I haven't done as well as I expected. What can I do now?

First of all, talk to your subject teacher. After all the teaching, tests and internal examinations that you have had, he/she is the person who best knows what grade you are capable of achieving. Take your results slip to your subject teacher, and go through the information on it in detail. If you both think there is something wrong with the result, the school or college can apply to see your completed examination paper and then, if necessary, ask for a re-mark immediately. The original mark can be confirmed or lowered, as well as raised, as a result of a re-mark.

How do my grades compare with those of everybody else who sat this exam?

You can compare your results with those of others in the UK who have completed the same examination using the information on the Edexcel website accessed at www.heinemann.co.uk/hotlinks (express code 4240P) by clicking on Edexcel.

I achieved a higher mark for the same unit last time. Can I use that result?

Yes. The higher score is the one that goes towards your overall grade. Even if you sat a unit more than twice, the best result will be used automatically when the overall grade is calculated. You do not need to ask the exam board to take into account a previous result. This will be done automatically so you can be assured that all your best unit results have gone into calculating your overall grade.

What happens if I was ill over the period of my examinations?

If you become ill before or during the examination period you are eligible for special consideration. This also applies if you have been affected by an accident, bereavement or serious disturbance during an examination.

If my school has requested special consideration for me, is this shown on my Statement of Results?

If your school has requested special consideration for you, it is not shown on your results slip, but it will be shown on a subject mark report that is sent to your school or college. If you want to know whether special consideration was requested for you, you should ask your Examinations Officer.

Can I have a re-mark of my examination paper?

Yes, this is possible, but remember that only your school or college can apply for a re-mark, not you or your parents/carers. First of all, you should consider carefully whether or not to ask your school or college to make a request for a re-mark. It is worth knowing that very few re-marks result in a change to a grade – not because Edexcel is embarrassed that a change of marks has been made, but simply because a re-mark request has shown that the original marking was accurate. Check the closing date for re-marking requests with your Examinations Officer.

When I asked for a re-mark of my paper, my subject grade went down. What can I do?

There is no guarantee that your grades will go up if your papers are re-marked. They can also go down or stay the same. After a re-mark, the only way to improve your grade is to take the examination again. Your school or college Examinations Officer can tell you when you can do that.

How many times can I re-sit a unit?

You may re-sit a modular GCSE Science or Mathematics module test once, prior to taking your terminal examination and before obtaining your final overall grade. The highest score obtained on either the first attempt or the re-sit counts towards your final grade. If you enter a module in GCSE Mathematics at a different tier, this does not count as a re-sit. If you are on the full modular Religious Studies GCSE course, and sat the first unit last year, you may re-sit module 1 when you sit module 2 to maximise your full course grade.

For much more information, go to www.heinemann.co.uk/hotlinks (express code 4240P) and click on examzone.

Glossary

This is an extended glossary containing definitions that will help you in your studies. Edexcel key terms are not included as all of these are defined in the lessons themselves.

abortion – The deliberate termination of a pregnancy, resulting in the death of the foetus.

ascension – When Jesus, after the resurrection, left his **apostles** and was carried up to **Heaven**.

Ash Wednesday – the first day of **Lent**, named after the tradition of applying a cross of ash to the forehead of Christians in church on Ash Wednesday.

baptism – A sacrament in which water is blessed and then poured over the head of a person, usually an infant, to represent the washing away of **sin** and the beginning of a new life with God.

Baptist Churches – Group of nonconformist churches committed to believer's baptism and the idea that all believers are priests.

CAFOD – Originally then known as the Catholic Fund for Overseas Development, nowadays the Catholic Agency for Overseas Development: a Roman Catholic charity.

celibacy – Living without engaging in any sexual activity.

Christian Aid – International charity dedicated to overcoming poverty, formed by the major Christian churches in the United Kingdom and Ireland.

Church of England – **Protestant** church formed by Henry VIII during the **Reformation**.

confession – admitting to your sins: for Roman Catholics, the sacrament of **reconciliation** is a formal act of confession to a priest.

Confirmation – Sacrament in which people confirm for themselves the promises made for them in infant baptism.

creationism – the literal belief that the story of Creation told in the book of Genesis is true. Creationists are opposed to **evolution**.

Easter Sunday – Last day of Holy Week, on which the resurrection occurred.

evolution – The gradual development of species over millions of years.

fasting – Willingly abstaining from some or all food, drink, or both, for a period of time, in order to achieve atonement for sins and to provide an opportunity for focus on the spiritual.

fundamentalism – The belief that the Bible is fact; that it is true in every way. **Creationism** is an important part of fundamentalism.

Golden Rule – Rule shared by most of the world's religions, states that we should treat others as we would want to be treated ourselves.

Good Friday – The day of Jesus' **crucifixion**.

Holy Spirit – The third person of the Trinity, equal with God the Father and God the Son. Christians talk more about God the Father and Jesus, God the Son, than about the Holy Spirit because the Holy Spirit works in ways that are less obvious.

Holy Week – Week beginning with **Palm Sunday** and ending on **Easter Sunday**.

inter-faith dialogue – Communication between different Christian faiths, and between Christianity and other religions.

Last Supper – Final meal Jesus shared with his **disciples**.

Lent – Period of preparation and prayer for 40 days before **Holy Week**.

liberalism – Set of beliefs which rejects **fundamentalism** and accepts the teachings of modern science.

Literalism – Form of **fundamentalism**, which believes that every word of the Bible is important and true.

Magisterium – The Pope and the bishops of the Roman Catholic Church.

Marriage – The condition of a man and woman being legally united for the purpose of living together and usually having children.

Maundy Thursday – Thursday in **Holy Week**, the day on which the **Last Supper** took place.

Methodism – A branch of **Protestant** Christianity that came into existence through the work of John Wesley in the 18th century.

Palm Sunday – The first day of **Holy Week**, named because of the palms used to cover the street Jesus rode into Jerusalem on.

parable – A story used to illustrate a moral or spiritual lesson.

Pentecost – When the **Holy Spirit** came down upon the **apostles**, after the **ascension** of Jesus.

Pentecostal Church – Group of Non-Conformist Churches that emphasise charismatic worship and personal experience of God through the **baptism** and the **Holy Spirit**.

pilgrimage – A journey undertaken for spiritual reasons: often a journey to a shrine or holy place.

Protestant – That part of the Christian Church that became distinct from the Roman Catholic and other churches, when their members 'protested' the centrality of the Bible and other beliefs.

Quakers – Nonconformist group also known at the Religious Society of Friends, characterised by informal worship with no priests or leaders and an emphasis on peaceful, simple living.

reconciliation – Roman Catholic sacrament in which people are freed from sins committed after receiving Baptism.

Reformation – Movement in the 15th and 16th centuries, when many believed that leaders of the Church had gone astray and broke away to form new Churches.

Salvation Army – Christian charity which seeks to bring food and shelter as well as Christian salvation to the poor and hungry.

sin – An action which is against God's rules.

symbolism – The use of symbols to represent ideas and emotions.

Ten Commandments – Set of rules given by God to Moses.

United Reformed Church – **Protestant** church formed from 1972 onwards by the union of Non-Conformist churches of the United Kingdom.

Index

In the following index, Edexcel key terms are given in **bold** and the first page number, also in bold, will lead you to the definition. For further definitions of unfamiliar words, see also the Glossary on pages 130.